Voices across the Water

Voices across the Water

An Anglo-Canadian Boyhood

Sydney Checkland

ABERDEEN UNIVERSITY PRESS
Member of the Maxwell Macmillan Pergamon Publishing Group

First published 1989
Aberdeen University Press
© Olive Checkland 1989

British Library Cataloguing in Publication Data

Checkland, S. G. (Sydney George), *1916-1986*
    Voices across the water: an Anglo-Canadian boyhood
    1. Canada. Social life. *1911–1935*. Biographies
    I. Title
    971.061′092′4

    ISBN 0 08 037972 9

Typeset from author-generated discs
and printed by AUP Glasgow/Aberdeen—A member of BPCC Ltd.

Contents

Illustrations

Foreword
Falaise, Normandy, August 1944

It was the Padre who found me lying on the soil of Normandy, there beside the burnt out tank, one of the casualties of the Canadian Armoured Division's struggle to close the pincer of the Falaise Gap. As he bent over me and I returned to consciousness his clerical collar, muddied and stained as it was, caught the sunlight. The sense of relief was overwhelming. The fear, the nausea, the feeling of slipping away was replaced by a soaring determination to live. I would return to England to wife and child, as yet unborn.

During that long August night, sliding very often from consciousness, the years of childhood and young manhood had all passed before me. In the following pages I have tried to remember the scenes which seemed so immediate as I lay wounded and helpless on foreign soil.

The ambulancemen, too spent to utter platitudes, cautiously bundled me up onto their stretcher, administered the morphine and carried me off.

Note on the Author

Sydney Checkland was born and brought up in Ottawa, Canada. In 1938—at the age of 22—he came to University in England. In 1944 he was severely wounded in Normandy and was invalided out of the Canadian Army. He served in the Universities of Liverpool and Cambridge before—in 1956—taking up the post of Professor of Economic History in the University of Glasgow. He was a distinguished historian whose books include *Scottish Banking* and *The Upas Tree*—on Glasgow. He was a Fellow of the British Academy and a Fellow of the Royal Society of Edinburgh. This present work has been prepared for publication by Olive Checkland.

CHAPTER 1

Canada and England

There has always been a powerful feeling, engendered no doubt by hearing my parents talk, that I was there with them on Parliament Hill in February 1916 as they stood in the snow on a freezing Ottawa night and watched the Canadian Houses of Parliament burn. It was a Wagnerian scene, as the fire mounted up the Gothic tower to burst forth from the four faces of the clock while the great bells, having struck midnight, broke from their burning timbers and crashed earthward, to be followed shortly by great chunks of the masonry itself. I was born in October 1916.

In spite of the crowds my parents were in a sense alone. They had come to Canada some two years before, newly married, immigrants from England. Sydney was 36 years old and Fanny 34. Both had intended to marry someone else and to remain English, in England. But my father had been finally rejected, and my mother's fiancé had died of tuberculosis. My older brother Edward, aged some seven months, lay in the dresser drawer that served for a cot, in the care of the landlady where they lodged. My parents were still wrapped in the reserve which was so common among incomers of the English lower middle classes. My father had as yet no real job. He was a *colporteur* for the Bible Society of Canada, responsible for distributing the Scriptures to the farmers and citizens of the small towns in the Ontario bush between the Ottawa River, the St. Lawrence and the Huron country. He had earlier done the same task along the Nova Scotia shore.

Both parents were intensely English. In my father's case particularly there was a strong puritan streak, for his mind was a curious mixture of pietism and the urge for rational comprehension. He believed (or thought he believed) in 'the truth, whithersoever it leadeth.' But he clung to the Bible as the irrefragable word of God. There could be no collision between the 'truth', however scientific, and the Bible. Maintaining this position in youth had caused him much agonised searching and thought, and still did.

We were to grow up with much of the strength and prejudice of puritan England of the seventeenth century, where, carried to Canada, it set the tone of our home. In the Canadian world outside, this belief

1

in righteousness was to meld uneasily with a society in which there was a casual cynicism about public men and their rectitude. Father, carrying to the British new world the stern spirit of the nonconformity of the old, had been conditioned into an obsessional drive to seek out authority, and under the influence of the imp of perversity, to attack it. This earned him a kind of wry respect in some quarters but made trouble for him throughout his life. He believed profoundly in England's civilising mission in the world—in short he was an imperialist, intensely loyal to the country he had deserted, and to whose establishment he had declared his enmity. He was an autodidact who had made himself something of an intellectual, but in argument he showed the pounding certitude of the self-taught, hinting at self-doubt.

Mother knew all this in her intuitive way and, when we reached the age of argument, would mediate between her husband and her sons. She buffered father's perversity and held private sessions with us in which she gave her own, less compulsive, view of life. 'You must not mind your father', she would say, 'you know he means well.' She was a Wesleyan Methodist, a nonconformist too, but not one afflicted with perversity as he was.

They had met in Winnipeg in the summer of 1914, while he was returning eastward across Canada and she was serving as a visiting sister in the National Children's Home there. A semi-courtship had taken place there, full of discretion and reservations. But on return to England contact had been made and a compact had been sealed, namely that they should return to Canada as man and wife. She had abandoned a career; he had left a clerkship without real prospects.

When our parents arrived in Ottawa there were nickelodeons—cheap cinemas—in Sparks Street. The lumber town that Queen Victoria had chosen as the seat of Canadian government, was taking its first steps from being a sawdust capital towards Sir Wilfrid Laurier's aspiration that it should become the 'Washington of the North'. The Ottawa Improvement Commission had been formed to bring this about. Right down to the Second World War, however, this aspiration was still remote. We were certainly not on the international circuit. Rare indeed were visitors from London, Paris, Vienna, Berlin or even Washington. There was little for them there. Despite our capital status, we had no theatre, concert hall or orchestra, no worthy National Gallery, no great national monuments. Indeed viewed on the international scale, the capital of Canada was hicksville. But we did have the Carnegie Library, the Dominion Experimental Farm, the Ottawa Senators hockey team (which did well in the National Hockey League against the Americans), and the Royal Canadian Mounted Police.

In a sense London was the model for Ottawa, providing an important

1   Sydney Tom Checkland and Fanny Selina Savory Mason, the author's
parents, Ottawa, Canada 1915.

element to the background of our growing up. Our Parliament buildings were modified British Victorian Gothic. Their dominance of the city skyline was secured by a byelaw limiting the height of the city's buildings to nine storeys, although as yet there was little threat of this. There was a tiny vice-regal court at Rideau Hall which was the focus of a minor diplomatic corps that followed the stiff precedents set in London at the Court of St. James'. The Governor-General, an ornament of the British aristocracy and sometimes royal, rode in state to open parliament and to read the Address from the Throne. The daughters of Ottawa's leading families, as debutantes, 'came out' at Rideau Hall. The Governor General's Foot Guards wore the bearskins, scarlet tunics and twin buttons of the Coldstream Guards, parading their colour as in London. The Princess Louise Dragoon Guards with their helmets, cuirrasses and swords provided a household cavalry, though these men, like the Foot Guards, were in fact week-enders, and not professional soldiers. The only assertion of distinctly Canadian ceremonial identity was that of the Royal Canadian Mounted Police with their famous headgear, but even they wore the scarlet tunics of Victoria's regiments of the line and demonstrated their horsemanship by lancing the tent pegs as Victoria's cavalry officers had learnt to do in India.

There were strong monarchist feelings. When Edward VIII abdicated in 1936 Canada was consulted and played its part in the deliberations that sent him packing, and was conscious that it had exchanged one king for another. Justice was dispensed in the King's courts and the mails were carried in the King's name, with the sign royal on the scarlet post boxes, universal symbols of the only monarchy in the Americas, intriguing to our few American visitors. The Imperial Order of the Daughters of the Empire thrived, cherishing a dream unimpaired by the rising idea of the Commonwealth. Civic ceremonial, like the national, followed the British precedent, with a mayoral chain, fur decked robes and tricorn hats. The older core of the city paid tribute (though a largely forgotten one) to the great of Britain and the imperial proconsuls of the past who filled the history books of the Province of Ontario. This was done by the naming of streets, schools and public places, perpetuating Carleton, Wellington, Victoria (Queen Street), Prince Albert, Metcalfe, Dalhousie, Elgin, Lisgar, Lansdowne and Minto, not to mention the English and Scottish counties of Kent, Somerset, Sussex, Cumberland and Argyll. Even in French Lower Town English place names predominated.

At a deeper level, too, the British influence was very powerful. In education the province of Ontario followed 'English'—really Scottish—models, a reflection of their strength in the Canadian universities, built in from the days of Upper and Lower Canada. The Universities,

McGill in Montreal, founded by James McGill (1744-1813) a University of Glasgow 'Student in Arts', and Queens in Kingston, were both largely Scottish foundations. The history and literature taught in the schools was largely British, with relatively little concession to the United States. So too with religion. Ottawa was dotted with protestant churches of the various sects, faithfully reproducing the traditions, architecture, idiosyncracies, divisions and zealotry of England, Scotland and Ireland. From Ulster had come the Loyal Orange Order with its fife and drum parades, its sashes and bowler hats together with its ancient anti-Catholic enmity centred on King Billy and the Battle of the Boyne. The Masonic Lodges were strongly English or Scottish: father detested their secret allegiances and caballistic practices. Within the Roman Catholic Church the powerful influence of Ireland, so long under British rule, contended for supremacy with the Catholicism of French Canada: for both of these father cherished the fear and revulsion of a puritan.

British culture in Ottawa was marginally challenged by the French. The Basilique Notre Dame d'Ottawa and other large grey limestone churches with their silver spires and crosses against the sky brought a touch of the distinctive architecture of the Province of Quebec. When a French-Canadian church was holding a bazaar there would be a large sign or banner outside it bearing the word 'Kermesse', invoking a distant echo of peasant life. In Lower Town the Byward Market conveyed something of *habitant* Canada, especially while the sleighs survived. French Canadians, living in Lower Town and in Hull ('ull) across the river, were a good deal less prosperous than most Anglo-Scots, carrying for us connotations of quaintness and perhaps failure to respond to the modern world. They were archaic exotics who mixed French and English as in 'Salon de Pool'. Byward Market was a place to which farmers and their wives came from the Upper Gatineau with their carts and sleighs, but increasingly with trucks and cars. They could, as the market ended, be haggled downward for their remaining chickens and other produce, for they needed cash and longed to leave the bitter winter day. The buildings surrounding the market were often of clapboard. They had no claim to distinction, but together composed an atmospheric whole, with overtones of a French Canadian village. This was Ottawa's only claim to the peasant picturesque. There were small shops, second hand stores and taverns with spittoons (these *crachoirs* we always associated with French-Canadians). You could catch occasional glimpses of *Le Droit*, a newspaper founded by the French community of the Oblate Order to defend the rights and to preserve the culture of the French speaking Roman Catholics. Lower Town had its French film houses, especially the *François*, though we never had the nerve or the inclination to enter them.

The architecture of Mansard and the Second Empire had come in the 1870s and 80s to Ottawa with the city hall, the Russell Hotel and the Langevin Block. But it was necessary to reach back further for the roots of French Canada. It was railway and official architecture that combined to bring the chateau style to the city, beginning with the Chateau Laurier in 1912 and spreading to the Confederation Building. This French component of the secular townscape of the capital was not the result, in the first instance, of any deep official sense of cultural appropriateness: the Chateau Laurier was to have continued the Gothic Revival style of Parliament Hill, but a strong-minded general manager of the Grand Trunk Railway decided, presumably on commercial grounds, to give Ottawa a new idiom, linking it with the chateaux of the Loire and the France of Samuel de Champlain. Town planning was, for us, a French speciality; Ottawa used the services of M. Gréber.

The third influence was the American, and in some ways it was the strongest. The houses occupied by modest families along downtown Ottawa's tree-lined streets were indistinguishable from those of an eastern American town. Indeed it was as if small-town America came to within a few blocks of the precinct of the national parliament. The verandah or porch was a feature of the more modest homes, with rails to sit on or to support your feet as you tilted your chair back. The verandah was a kind of observers' podium, set a foot or so above ground level, often with rocking chairs for the senior members of the family, where grandparents could be safely installed for hours. It was a place floored and roofed with wood, linking the house to the world of neighbours and passers-by in summer, but bleakly deserted in winter. The rectangular business buildings were also in a shared American idiom, often in red brick with prominent iron fire escapes. The street cars were in the American style. In a sense even the Chateau Laurier and its pseudo-French imitators were Yankee buildings, having rectangular steel frames merely capped by the French motif. For money we used dollars and cents and as the currencies of the United States and Canadian were then at par it was easy to identify with Americans.

The movie houses that spread so fast in the early 1920s from the United States were highly derivative: the greatest of them, Loews (later the Capital), opened in 1920. Though its foyer with its mirrors seemed so palatial to a child, it was a mass-produced movie house, part of a chain made possible ultimately by the pogroms of Tsarist Russia and eastern Europe which had released the energies of these immigrant movie moguls of America, creators of the American dream. When in our history class we reached the Hall of Mirrors at Versailles it was Loew's foyer and mezzanine that sprang to mind. These darkened worlds of black and white shadows, showing silent films in our preadolescence, taken together with radio programmes, the phonograph, the syndicated newspaper features (including Dorothy Dix, the agony aunt) and the 'funnies' (the comic strips), brought to us the American way of life, partly in reality and partly in caricature. They were con-firmed by the wise-cracking idiom of vaudeville, the songs of Tin-Pan Alley, the Jazz of the American negro south and the Jewish wit of New York. Ottawa business men eagerly joined the proliferating service clubs, satirised in Sinclair Lewis' novel *Babbitt*, especially the Rotary and the Lions.

The Canadian breed of politician, who with his bureaucrats provided the economic base of Ottawa, though he followed British ritual and procedures on Parliament Hill, was essentially American in idiom and in outlook. Like his American counterpart, he was often a long-distance railway traveller. He would emerge unshaven from his sleeper into Union Station opposite the Chateau Laurier, always aware that in a country cobbled together on a continental scale political power and survival sprang from the manipulation and reconciliation of regional differences of interest and outlook. Any Canadian cabinet was largely the outcome of political bargaining on this basis. The speech of the Ottawa Valley had for a generation or more lost touch with the babel of European accents of the pioneering days, and had been flattened out into a form of American. But there was still a degree of distinctive sound which contained trace elements of the Irish and the Scots.

In short, the ways of everyday secular life were strongly affected by emanations from the United States as its manifest destiny advanced it to the forefront of the nations. America, of course, like Britain and France, was moved by its own self-engrossed dynamics. Its effects on Canada were sheer inadvertance, an overlapping into a peripheral market. But beneath this in the Canadian consciousness there moved the twin European heritages of Britain and France, not homogenised as in the United States, but distinct and self-conscious, from which derived religion, education, ceremonial, architecture and a sense of distinctiveness, though not of solidarity.

But in 1916 as my parents watched the burning of the Parliament Buildings, my father was certainly thinking of the war in Europe. Could the Germans have done this terrible thing? Canadians at the time flattered themselves that the Kaiser and his war lords, in spite of pressing preoccupations in Europe, had incendiary designs on their government and its buildings. The war had been going on for nearly two years, causing Canadian soldiers to be sent to France, raising the fearful spectre of conscription, so fiercely rejected by French Canadians, and making father wonder if he too, in spite of his age and family, should offer himself. He had no doubt that the war was a just one and

2   Private Sydney Tom Checkland, volunteer in the Canadian Army, 1917.

that the Germans must be stopped at whatever cost. He believed in the German atrocities in Belgium, assiduously spread by the Allied propaganda machine. Europe was calling him back.

In October 1917, when I was one year old, father disappeared for eighteen months. He volunteered to serve in France with the 207th Ottawa Regiment. He was responding to the call of England as much as that of Canada. He left mother, encumbered by two small sons, to face the loneliness and uncertainty of an alien country on an army wife's pay.

Perhaps going to war was for him an escape, offering the exhilaration of physical fitness and of a popular even an heroic role. In any case come what may he would see England again. Killing and being killed were kept remote and unreal by the euphoria of commitment to the cause of civilisation. Mother had known for some time that he had been edging towards a decision. In the end she said 'Go, if you feel you must'. He was thirty-seven years of age.

She feared greatly for him. He might die in battle. He might return shattered in body or mind. Whatever happened she knew he would confront those in authority. He was, she knew, stubborn (he called it integrity), and his independence of spirit always caused trouble. These would make the army for him not merely a vehicle of war against the Germans, but also for confrontation with those set in authority over him. This latter, lesser, fear was indeed born out. Twice he was raised to the rank of sergeant and then reduced to private, though he achieved sergeant again in the end. His first such elevation, given while still serving in Ottawa, was largely a reward for setting up and editing a regimental newspaper, called *The Whizzbang*. Hardly had this been achieved when he was demoted for using the paper as a vehicle to criticise officers' privileges and behaviour. He deplored the free access, which commissioned officers had, to the City of Hull over the Ottawa river in Quebec, where among the French Canadians there was liquor that was prohibited in Ottawa itself. On the occasion of his second demotion he was in military hospital in England recovering from wounds and internal haemorrhaging after Passchendaele. He insisted on keeping books on his bedside table despite the hospital rule that such space be kept clear. Poor mother, at home in Ottawa, bore the brunt of these acts of defiance, for her pay as a soldier's wife rose and then fell with each demotion.

On other scores she had no cause to worry. He was the strictest of teetotalers who knew not the taste of alcohol, an ardent supporter of the Prohibition then operating in Ontario. He refused the rum issue on the battlefield, calling it dastardly, believing that death or maiming should be met with a clear head and eye. His intense evangelical

upbringing had innoculated him absolutely against womanising. He
was impervious to invitations which said 'Come on Syd, why not take
your fun when you can get it—you may never get back.' Of pros-
titution he took a characteristically 'logical' view, 'If', he said, 'it is
argued that men in the forces need women for this purpose, why do
your wives and daughters not volunteer?' The army company most
congenial to him was that of the chaplains, the only source of any
kind of cultured conversation. But he could not forebear telling them,
as ordained men and commissioned officers, how little they really knew
of the lives of their men.

Mother suffered great loneliness and a sense of abandonment. Her
friends were usually English women of her own generation long resi-
dent in Canada. In after years mother tended to rank her friends on a
scale related to their wartime treatment of her. The fearful winters, so
unlike those of her west country upbringing in Bristol, with the intense
Canadian cold and heavy snow, weighed particularly heavily upon
her. Living in lodgings caused an uneasy nomadic feeling. She had
difficulty breast-feeding me; Allenbury's Baby Food came to the rescue.

There was, too, the longer perspective: what would happen when
the army no longer provided secure employment for her husband?
When she was approached by a share-pusher with an offer of an
investment in a gold mine she surrendered up a hundred dollars or so.
That a woman of such sound sense could do this was a reflection of
the effects on her of isolation and her desire to make the economic
future less threatening. The shares of course proved worthless. Her
mind ran on her corner of England—Bristol with the tramway centre,
Clifton with its suspension bridge, the Avon Gorge, the Downs, the
Wesleyan Chapel, and her actor brother George who had forever to be
sent money to get him home again, Painswick village churchyard in
Gloucestershire where her grandfather and grandmother Savory lay
under the elms also figured in her reveries. Did she also think of her
former career, which she had abandoned, with Dr. Barnardo and with
the National Children's Homes?

Father's homecoming was in April 1919. He carried his wound
stripe and his restored sergeant's rank. He had left not a few of his
comrades on Flanders' fields. Fate had saved him from the principal
slaughter of Passchendaele, for on the march from Boulogne to Etaples
to join the Princess Patricia's Canadian Light Infantry he had developed
blisters on his feet which turned sceptic. This delayed his arrival in the
trenches. But he had made his way into that muddy carnage, had
suffered nights of bombardment and had his Lewis machine gun
buckled on the parapet above his head before he was cut about with
shrapnel and started passing blood in his urine.

CHAPTER 2

Settling Down

Father's return from the war was celebrated by a photograph of the four of us, inspired partly by his sense of occasion, and partly by the desire to send pictures of his family to his brothers and sisters in England. Father stands proudly, his cap bearing the badge of the Princess Patricia's Canadian Light Infantry, sharing the distinguished record of his regiment. He was no longer an outsider in Canada, but carried a new status as a battle veteran. In the photograph he balances his younger son, aged two-and-a-half, on a kind of fern stand, while Eddie is independently on his feet. We were deeply wary of this stranger who had invaded our intimate life with our mother. We have matching sailor suits, our hat bands reading *Democracy*. Mother's face is taut with the strain of the years of separation and coping. There is moreover the stubborn question, how is a family of four to be supported now? The war gratuity of $600 seemed a large sum, but how long would it last? Father was by now nearly forty, with no real job in sight.

There seemed nothing for it but to go back to the Bible Society. They took him on, temporarily. They sent him to attend the annual meetings of branches in the district. He was to point out the moral of war experiences and to recount the value of the work done by the Society for the troops overseas. He also preached at scores of church services, taking as his text 'Redeeming the time, because the days are evil'. Only by a wider distribution and understanding of the word of God, he told congregations in the smaller Ontario towns, could the world be saved from the calamities that threatened it.

The desire to be useful, together with a sound instinct, led him to join the Great War Veterans' Association. Perhaps his reputation for challenging authority was somehow approved, for he was elected a Vice-President, the only non-officer in such a position. As unemployment threatened, one of the Association's main concerns was with the resettlement of soldiers. There were long and gruelling meetings and conferences, gradually diffused with a feeling of futility. Only economic prosperity could really deal with the problem of employment. In Canada, as elsewhere, there was a brief post-war boom, before the economy subsided into the slump of the early 1920s. A visit from the

11

3   Sergeant Checkland, Fanny, Edward and Sydney George, April 1919: the
boys' caps bear the legend 'Democracy'.

Prince of Wales to the Association brought great satisfaction. Our living room was adorned by a group photograph showing father in the company of the Prince. But there was no solution to post-war unemployment.

For our father relief was at hand. Someone noticed him using his shorthand, in which he was a self-taught expert. He was asked to teach it in a Vocational Training School for veterans. To mother's great relief there was now an income. But father found the boredom stupefying, with hour after hour of Pitman's pothooks.

There was one last bid he could make for a job that would allow him a degree of fulfilment. This was journalism. He had done a little of this as a free-lance aspirant in England, and had sent from England and France articles describing the Canadian forces abroad. These had been published by the *Ottawa Citizen*. This, together with his scrapbook of clippings of his writings from Birmingham papers, secured his entré as a reporter on the staff of the *Citizen*. When he said farewell to the Veterans' Vocational School he was presented with a splendid gold mounted and engraved Swan fountain pen which delighted him. He had seen similar pens advertised at Piccadilly Circus in London.

Though the money was less and the hours erratic, newspaperwork was what he wanted. It gave him a kind of freedom, together with a wide range of contacts and an opportunity to express himself. He assumed his 'beat' in Ottawa and district, variously consisting of the police station and the law courts, the School Board, the City Council, the churches, parliament, conventions, fires and other emergencies, the occasional newsworthy sermon, and national occasions, together with, from time to time, the writing of feature articles and 'Saturday Specials'. In the first months or so as a reporter he put his contributions into a scrap book, revelling in the words he had written as he had done in England. But this practice soon faded as his self-confidence grew. Within a year he was a familiar figure in the *Citizen* newsroom, respected as a man who was deeply informed about Britain, who had travelled in Egypt and the Holy Land, who had crossed the United States and Canada and who had helped to see the Kaiser off. By the spring of 1923 he was covering the paper's biggest assignments, taking down verbatim Lloyd George's speech at the Royal Ottawa Golf Club soon after the Welsh Wizard had fallen from power. His new world gave opportunities, in words, to set the world to rights. Dad also achieved the unenviable reputation of harassing the city editor as he struggled under pressure to get a paper out.

The younger reporters were inclined to be patronising about this stern older fellow, who abhorred alcohol, gambling and womanising, and took little part in city room japes and jokes. In any case his conversation was imperialistic and his Baptist piety too much for many. He would stir the city room in his penetrating English voice with talk of what Curzon would have done in India, or what Keir Hardie stood for in the British Labour movement or Dean Inge in the Church of England. Lloyd George, his hero, was always a favourite subject. No one, it seems, was ever left in doubt about what Syd felt about anything. His colleagues, who shared the worldliness of their American counterparts, would sometimes revenge themselves on him by provocative remarks. One of them, knowing his feeling that cricket was almost a sacred rite, once said, 'Hey, Syd, what's that game they play in England with a big wooden spoon?' This question not only provoked a lecture on cricket, but also dark hints about North American baseball being clearly descended from English rounders.

But father soon earned respect 'on the beat'. He would walk into the office early, his blue suit set off by a red plaid tie flowing from his starched collar with rounded ends, grab a morning paper, sit down and devour it all. Then, late, he would jump up, rush out, and by dint of perseverance combined with skill, get caught up with the news around town. He would then enter upon phase two of his day, which combined typing up his items and holding forth to the city room.

This was to be Dad's professional persona through all the years of our growing up and early manhood. It was gradually revealed to us in small glimpses, especially on the rare occasions when we were taken to the *Citizen* office. The city room reverberated to the clatter of typewriters, shouted instructions, general conversation, telephone bells, cries of 'copy' to raise the copy boy, and the whoosh of the suction tubes that carried the copy down to the linotype men below. Dad was in his element in the city room. His contacts were maintained by a combination of sincerity, self-acquired erudition and the judicious use of favourable references. In his cynical moments he divided the Ottawa world, dominated by politicians and civil servants, into two classes of people, namely those anxious to get their names into the paper and those anxious to keep them out. He was never to be more than a street-pounding reporter and he was never to earn more than $2,000 per year.

Early in his newspaper career there had arisen an opportunity to join the Hansard staff on Parliament Hill, taking down the parliamentary debates. Father with his skill in shorthand could have gained security, freedom from tension, general respect and a good pension. But always a man to reject a safe routine, he turned the chance down, preferring the living world of his beat with its contacts and occasional excitements. As he aged, however, as the depression made jobs precarious, and as his crochets became more pronounced, being a newspaper man began to take its toll on him and on our mother.

His connection with the Great War Veterans Association ended. Such bodies, inevitably as the war receded, along with the sense of gratitude and admiration for its veterans, lost their momentum. In particular there was Dad's fierce hostility to alcohol, which had become the great consolation of many former comrades in arms who still used the veterans' clubs.

The urge for renewal faded on the national plane as well. One of father's early important assignments was to cover the Dominion Council set up by the National Conference on Character Education in Relation to Canadian Citizenship. Held in Winnipeg it was attended by 1,500 educationalists of all shades of opinion earnestly seeking a path to national regeneration. The voice of radicalism from western Canada opined that 'the prevailing emphasis on competitive methods in industry and commerce has tended to a weakening of the sense of solidarity among the citizens of Canada'. A National Council emerged but it too lost its way.

With a job with a living wage, and with the gratuity of $600 largely unspent, father's first thought was not better housing or any other long-term provisions, but a trip to the Old Country, a reward, as he put it, for mother for all her wartime loneliness. Late in October 1920 we all sailed for England, staying over Christmas. All my memories, (aged four and a half) have to do with mother's relatives and friends in Clifton, Bristol.

There was Auntie Evelyn, mother's elder sister, looking very like her, with the same features and the same English-rose complexion. Sadly her morose husband was already developing the miserly side of his character and making life difficult for all around him. Cousin Millie was a girlhood intimate: her father, Uncle Rick, had been a butler in one of the great houses of the West of England. There Fanny and Millie as children had loved to explore. It was especially exciting when the family was away and the vast entertaining rooms were dim behind their closed shutters and the furniture was ghostly under its dust covers. There was fearful Great Aunt Fanny, for whom mother had been named. She had entered the twilight world of senile dementia. With her wild eyes and the bristles round her mouth that stung when she levied her terrible tribute of a kiss she revolted and terrified us. Eddie with the wisdom of his almost six years assured me she was a witch.

Among these memories, no doubt strengthened by mother's later and somewhat wistful recall (it was the last time but one she saw England), there was Roger Mcqueen. He had come under her care some ten years earlier, in the National Children's Orphanage at the age of fifteen or so, both of his parents being suicides. When she left the Home he had given her a book of Shelley's poems. He was now prosperous, with his foot well placed on the ladder of business success. Dad believed, perhaps with some truth, that Roger had fallen in love with mother when he most needed love, and was so still. There were thirteen years between them. With father in London, Roger took the three of us to one of Bristol's pantomimes, *Tom, Tom the Piper's Son*. Two recollections remain, the one of mother's unease as the three of us, having arrived early at the theatre, waited; the other of Tom appearing holding a real live squealing piglet under his arm.

For father the call of London was as irresistible as always. He had loved walking its streets as a young man, having journeyed up by train from Birmingham in his top hat and frock coat. For him London was the centre of the universe, the scene of momentous events and the haunt of great men such as made Ottawa seem brash indeed. The urge to be in London near the great pulse of the Empire never left him. He was particularly moved by the ceremonies on Armistice Day, 11 November 1920 when the new gleaming Cenotaph in Whitehall was unveiled and the burial of the Unknown Warrior took place in Westminster Abbey. He attained a high exaltation as, from beside the Admiralty Arch, he saw the gun carriage bearing the coffin of the Warrior approach along the Mall and pass on to the Abbey, to the heavy tempo of the slow march played by the bands of the Brigade of Guards and accompanied by the victorious generals, admirals and air marshals. The procession was headed by Field Marshall, the Earl Haig.

But reality for the four of us now lay in Canada: for Dad the life of a newspaperman, for mother that of a homemaker, for Eddie, school and for me an interval before initiation into that alien world where the tone was to be set by Canadian kids and their teachers.

With Eddie banished by day I had mother to myself. The ages between four and five are the last phase of security within the nest. The world is on the four-to-five-year-old scale—composed of adults so much larger than oneself. The infant eyeball level is so low: it scanned a world of watch chains and waist-coats and suits that were usually blue, of ladies laps, of table tops and dressing tables requiring a stretching of toes (but the contents of which were forbidden to the touch), of hymn racks in church pews on which you banged your head, of adult hands to be clutched or evaded, so different as between men and women. Occasional visits to public urinals in the company of father brought the stink of strong male urine close to nose and mouth. Mysterious adult utterances that one knew held important secrets were picked up, but wrapped in circumlocutions because 'little jugs have big ears'. I dimly recall asking mother what her breasts were for, the memory being underlined because of the laughter when she retold the story. There was the puzzling question of the manual dexterity of parents: both of them could get at least another spoonful out of a boiled egg after you had thought there could be no more. You saw your mother's corsets for the last time just before being expelled to school. It was your final chance to share an afternoon nap with her, watching her bosom rise and fall. Few nightmares survive in memory, though there was one that was fearful indeed, inspired by the sight under a great flat stone, that father in his educational way had lifted, of lizard-like, revolting purple-grey rubberoid creatures of the dark, blind and languid, but stirring slightly as if preparing to release some nameless evil directed at me alone.

Mother with her skill learned in the clothing factory in Bristol was adept at the sewing machine and so could save money by making much of our clothing. As winter approached she made us each a coat that would have passed without comment, except that she had sewn to the collars strips of fur, thinking this highly suitable for a Canadian winter. This was for some reason thought by our classmates to be incongruous, giving rise to the school-yard cry of 'Rats' tails!' The fur incident meant the abandonment of protective anonymity needed by a shy and timid child. Even so sensitive and experienced a person as our mother did not identify this fear of the herd and it was impossible to tell her. Eventually after long and tearful battles in which father spoke darkly of ingratitude, she sadly removed the loathsome fur she had thought so fine.

Neither parent understood the challenge that faced us, being so palpably 'English' among so many seemingly confident Canadian kids. Certainly there were others of various and more exotic ethnic origins in the class, but in some ways their problems of assimilation were less than ours. They were braced for the challenge in a way that we were not. Our city home was very English, withdrawn and self-contained. We made few close friends. Our parents never really assimilated to the neighbourhood, maintaining a distant politeness in the English middle class manner. We were told to come straight home after school and were kept strictly 'off the streets'. The result was that we never bonded with a gang of other kids and so failed to gain social cunning or access to that world of things that parents do not know that you know.

We now had rooms in the upper part of the house of Mr. and Mrs. Wilkie. They too were English. Mr. Wilkie was a skilled man, a gas fitter, with all the practicality with his hands that our Dad lacked. He was master of the furnace, knowing how to feed it, deal with its temperament, adjust its draughts, shake out its ashes—in short perform the basic Canadian winter cellar tasks that father, raised in small English open-fire houses, usually tended by his sisters, could never do. Mr. Wilkie, as trainer, manager and coach of the Sons of England soccer team, was a wizard at blowing up and lacing a ball, doing so with a skill that seemed to us miraculous, producing a rock-like sphere with a high bounce. This large-handed man with his broken nose, an escapee from the English working class, assimilated to Canada in a way that father, in England a respectable clerk, could not. So too with Mrs. Wilkie. She was a small wiry person with sharp eyes and ears and a kind heart, who knew the women of the neighbourhood, entertaining them on a modestly lavish scale in her hot kitchen and passing on to our mother such of the local gossip as she thought appropriate.

As the perils of school were lessened by experience and guile it began to have its attractions. The teachers, mostly women, enjoyed their classes of still cuddly and often comical kids. Home and school became daily reciprocals, each with its own concerns, with each world kept separate from the other. One did not babble to schoolmates about home affairs. Though we brought the drawings, cardboard creations, weavings and other products of our supervised school ingenuity home to our parents (one learned quite early to doubt the critical faculties of one's parents as they lavished praise on our modest efforts), we said less and less about what happened in the classroom and in the schoolyard and in those parts of school where there was no supervision, partly for fear of provoking parental intervention.

In the winter city there was the smell of a heavy fall of snow and the sight of a newly virginal world. There were horse-drawn sleighs, their bells singing sweetly as on their gracefully curved runners they swept their fur-clad occupants through the snowy streets. Unfortunately in my childhood these romantic carriages were fast yielding to the new automobiles with their clank of loose snow chains on their mudguards and the stink of their antifreeze. Along the streetcar tracks the snow was cleared by gangs of men with shovels loading Ford tip-up trucks, working with great speed. There were special streetcars which had enormous rotating bamboo brushes on their bows. When the bristles fell out they were quickly harvested by small boys. Armed with a bamboo bristle you could try to smash another's overcoat buttons. The trick was to hold the bottom end of the stick with your left hand, bend it back with the right and release it smack onto the button. There were other winter hazards. The fearful cold could quickly freeze an exposed ear making it sting and swell to a painful red and rubbery condition which finally peeled. And as the snow melted there was the extraordinary discovery that the footpath had wandered about so that when workmen cut channels to the sewers we found we had been walking on the edge of the road. The spring slush had, for us as children, its squelchy joys.

Though horses were being pushed out in the 1920s, they still held a place in our lives, though few city children had ever touched, much less handled one. They were still part of our speech as when one boy would dismiss a statement by another as 'horseballs'. There was an annual horse parade with their plaited manes and tails, rosettes and ribbons, glittering brasses, polished harness, flowers and resplendent carts. Very occasionally a runaway horse would clatter along the street, free of its master and so terrified that the whites of its eyes would show, its cart rocking and bumping behind it, the reins dragging along the road. A horse would sometimes fall on an icy street, especially on an incline, gathering a small crowd. Its head would curve upward as it struggled to rise, its flailing ironshod hooves striking sparks from the granite setts.

In winter our small family turned in upon itself, especially at weekends and particularly on Sundays. Yet, because of the nature of Dad's job as a journalist, his interests and his anxieties did convey something of Canadian and even of international affairs to us as soon as we showed any interest. In one way we lived at the centre of Ottawa affairs, privy to inside information about all manner of public matters. At an early age we listened to Dad's accounts of how he had penetrated various conspiracies of silence by politicians, local and national. Our home in downtown Ottawa was always within easy walk of the newspaper office and his 'beat', together with Parliament Hill and the Chateau Laurier, those two foci of Canadian policy making.

When I was six-years-old my brother and I awoke to find father sitting on our bed. 'Boys', he announced, 'you have a little brother!' A few days later on getting home from school we found that mother had reappeared from the nursing home, smiling and warm. Her long hair, usually so carefully arranged, was flowing down her back and she was holding the baby. At the age of forty-two she was committed once more to the close routine of motherhood. The baby's first name was to be Kenneth, the second Lloyd. This latter, together with my own middle name of George, celebrated father's political hero. The result of having no sisters was that mother was isolated with four males. There was a tendency on my part to idealise the female race, a weakness to which boys with sisters are immune.

There was little space in Mrs. Wilkie's upper rooms in Bay street in which to deploy the things that parents had brought from England, but little space was needed. The principal item was a sewing table that Dad had bought in Damascus. It was covered with inlays of various eastern woods (eighteen in all as he delighted to count them), together with mother-of-pearl and thin strips of silver. All of these had been tapped into place by child labour which had inspired in father a mixture of indignation at their exploitation and admiration for the skills of their small hands. Father had given the table to his wife as his wedding present—he had little else to give and what little money he still had had been needed for the Atlantic crossing. It stood in a corner of the room. The wooden case in which it had travelled from Damascus served as a cupboard, its front decently draped with a curtain.

On this sewing table, which was, of course, too precious to be used for sewing, standing on a lace doily, was a white plaster bust of Lloyd George. Inside, visible through the glass windows, stood a bowl and a horn beaker: these, all that mother had from her Bristol home, were reputed to be rare and valuable. In the same corner of the room hung a wall bracket, mostly inlaid with mother of pearl from the same Damascus factory. On it stood a brown plaster bust of Sir Wilfrid Laurier. Thus did the respective giants of British and Canadian Liberalism, both of whom father was proud to have met, share our domestic shrine. Sir Wilfrid, though denied priority of place, was in the end luckier, for Eddie in one disastrous moment knocked Lloyd George from his pedestal. He broke into a thousand pieces. This happened just about the time when, to father's great indignation, the British Tories had toppled Lloyd George from the prime ministership by conspiring at the Carlton Club in faraway London. The Welsh wizard was never to rise again.

Beside Sir Wilfrid's bracket hung a beaded fly whisk, also from the East. Disposed variously around the walls were Bible texts, on cardboard, as supplied by the Bible Society. They included 'As for Me and my House, we will serve the Lord', and 'Thou, God, seest me', the latter was illuminated by a vast single dilated eye. There was also a large framed photograph of the S.S. *Olympic* which had served as a troopship, carrying father to the war.

A vast family Bible of some age had been acquired at second hand in Canada so that someone else's family inscriptions were covered by a carefully glued-in sheet of paper. On it father had written in his best hand with his Swan fountain pen our names and the dates of birth of we boys (parental ages were a carefully guarded secret), while mother had inserted locks of our baby hair tied with thread. The heavy gilt-edged pages had to be turned with reverential care. Father would tell us the stories featured in the illustrations. He liked especially, looking up at his wife, to recount that of Ruth, and how she had said to Boaz, 'Whither thou goest, I will go, and where thou dwellest I will dwell'.

The greatest treat of all was the Holyland bag, a leather affair of the kind named for Mr. Gladstone. It contained the things father had brought back from his eastern travels to illustrate his lectures and sermons, and which he had used in his Bible toting days in Nova Scotia and Ontario. He would get it out and slowly produce its contents, carefully allowing us to see only one item at a time while he told the full tale in each case. First came the fez from Egypt which he would wear throughout the performance. Then came two bottles of water, one from the River Jordan and the other from the Dead Sea. The metal cap of the latter was immovably fixed by corrosion, while inside was a murky fluid in which bits of solid matter of considerable size floated about. It was rather like one of those snowstorms inside glass paper-weights, but one which had somehow become defiled. Father would tell us of his party's dragoman who had likened certain men to the Dead Sea, for they received as did that Sea, but there was no outflow, so that the result was corruption. There was a miniature grindstone, about two inches across, made of some black stone, used to illustrate how in the Book of Ecclesiastes—at the Latter Day of Judgement two shall be grinding at the mill. One shall be taken and the other left. There were bits of husk of the kind which the prodigal son in his extremity fain would share with the swine, though these were in an advanced stage of disintegration. Then came the yashmak, a black veil for Muslim women with a curious metal cylinder that lay along the bridge of the nose, with two serrated rings around it, intended said father, to ward off the evil eye. Primitive snapshots showed father with his Cook's tour companions, on the ruins at Baalbek or insecurely seated on camels with the Sphynx and the pyramids of Cheops as background. Finally, and best of all, there was a sling bought from a hunchbacked pedlar of the kind that David had used to slay Goliath. I doubt that Dad had ever really tried to cast a pebble from it, but he delighted to stand, his feet braced, the fez incongruously on his head, the ends of the two thongs of the sling held between thumb and forefinger, whirling it about his head as he declaimed Goliath's challenge, 'Am I a dog that you come out against me with staves?' Then, with a shout he would release one end of the sling so that the imaginary stone flew to pierce the massive skull of the Philistine. He would then sit down and recount how that, when he had preached in a chapel in a tiny Nova Scotia settlement the place was unexpectedly crowded. The rumour had spread since his afternoon appearance at the Sunday School that a man would preach that evening who had the sling that had killed Goliath.

In addition to these treasures father had a number of things stowed in and around his waistcoat. There was his gold watch chain, the pride of his days as a clerk in the Shropshire Union Railway and Canal Company. In the lower pocket on one side was a pair of folding scissors with which he could cut an item from the newspaper with an extraordinary deftness. On the other side in a tiny pouch was the gold guinea his favourite sister Louise had given him when as a soldier he had left England in 1917 for France. He had sworn to her he would never spend it. In one of the upper pockets was the tuning fork he had used to set the note for the singing in the Sunday School of which he had been secretary in Birmingham. These various objects of course took their toll of his waistcoats, causing shine and wear at the places where they bulged. His dark blue jacket was already gravely distorted by the wad of reporters' copy paper, which, folded once, he carried in its inside pocket along with letters and memos of various kinds.

Mother's box of photos was about eight inches by six and four inches deep, made of heavy linen, covered with faded green embroidery. It encompassed her life in England. There was Percy Boxwell, her dead fiancé who might have been our father, and Mrs. Boxwell his mother, a sprightly lady in widow's weeds unexpectedly lifting her voluminous skirts while skipping rope. There were excursion photos with mother so young, wide eyed in a wide brimmed hat, with leg-of-mutton sleeves. There was Uncle George in his various stage roles; in some, especially Shylock, wearing palpably false whiskers. Aunt Fanny was present, looking bright and responsive before her mind had darkened. The various orphanages where mother had served were represented, one picture showing the boys happily scrubbing the floors. Mother appeared in her uniform in various interior settings among the other sisters, pouring tea or chatting. These pictures carried for me the fascination of a past that was closed, full of the mystery of what had happened and what might have been. There was also a fine steel comb which mother had used on orphan boys to remove lice from their hair: if we were seen scratching our heads we knew it would at once be brought into vigorous play.

From as early as we could remember we knew that Jesus was our friend. We knelt by the bedside every night to say our prayers:

> *Gentle Jesus, meek and mild,*
> *Look upon a little child,*
> *Suffer me to come to thee,*
> *Pity my simplicity ...*

To this was added a special requests section. From the time I was seven or so there were family prayers on winter Sunday nights with father presiding in patriarchal fashion. When we were old enough we boys would take turns reading a passage from the Bible, by which means the splendid language and cadences of the King James version came to bury themselves deep within us.

Food was a gift from God, recognised as such by the grace said before every meal except breakfast, viz. 'We thank thee Lord for this our food, for life and health and every good' (often shortened to the first half). When I was about six I had an epic battle with father over supper (or 'tea' as we knew it). A crust of mine had somehow become dampened: I had an abhorrence of wet bread, related with all the intensity of childhood revulsion to once having seen Mr. Bagg the iceman at Britannia preparing the food for his pigs. This secret detestation of course could not be pleaded to justify an exemption. Long after my brother had been excused from the table, the three of us sat there in silence contemplating the awful crust. Finally mother broke the silence, quietly asking me to be a good boy. There was nothing for it but a quick grab and a gulp.

There was a panicky fear on my part that our prayers, our grace saying and other religiosities might come to the notice of our schoolmates. They would certainly use them for raillery. My older brother did not seem to share this dread. Indeed, in a bout of competitive boasting about Dads in the schoolyard when he was about nine, he had announced, quite rightly, that his father was a Deacon. He was astonished at the howls of derision this brought, together with the nickname 'Deac'. This he turned to advantage, accepting it and writing it as an addition to his name in his schoolbooks: it accompanied him through his school career.

The only point at which a small boy entered the world of men, apart from public urinals, was the barber shop. This was a place of mirrored walls, chairs that could be cranked up or down or made to recline, of sinks with hoses attached, of rows of scissors and clippers, shaving brushes and mugs, with shelves of hair tonics. Lifted onto a board placed across the arms of the chair you were elevated to the eye level of the barber and were subjected to an invasion of privacy that had no parallel. So much so that one of our friends refused point blank to go, obliging his mother to do her best on him in the kitchen for his father refused to face the panic scenes which could be produced if he were forced. The final stages of getting your hair cut were the use of the razor, after a strop or two, on the back of the neck, the sprinkling of sickly-sweet water followed by the stiff action of the barber's fingers on the scalp, the incised parting and the holding by the barber of a square mirror at the back of your head to provide a rear view, revealing your ears starting forth from your head without sheltering undergrowth. But there was the consolation that you were getting what the men got, namely 'short back and sides'. My first scary sense of the infinite came while sitting on the barber's board; it was inspired by the regression caused by the wall of mirrors reflecting that behind, sending their images deeper and deeper into one another without limit.

It was father, of course, who took us to the barbers, and it was a comfort to have him there. But it was his limitations that I became aware of long before those of mother. Perhaps this had something to do with deeply rooted things, a competitiveness with father not present with mother. The Kodak camera provided an early revelation of paternal frailty. He had bought this instrument, at second hand, being intrigued by the possibility of making his own pictures for the family record. They would be useful to send to his brothers and sisters in England. It was a large and heavy affair in a case which added considerably to its weight. When the front flap had been hinged down, you pulled a sort of bellows along miniature tracks until it checked into position. Father would study the angle of the sun. The subjects to be photographed would then be carefully instructed and posed. Then came the measuring of the exact distance, done by father turning his back on his subjects and then carefully placing heel to toe twelve times. There would be elaborate peerings through the camera's sights, followed by last minute instructions on position, posture and expression. Having taken the street car to Rockliffe Park one spring, mother and we three boys were almost eaten alive by mosquitoes while father, having put a ban on all movement, fussed about. The snapshots were the reward. These were always opened and viewed with care in a small family ceremony. Through the stiffness and artificiality could one see what the world saw of oneself?

CHAPTER 3

Early School Days

Mrs. Harrison, our kindergarten teacher at Slater Street Public School, was a bouncy matron of the callisthenics school, whose jollity overcame her sensitivity, making her very frightening to a nervous infant. On my first morning, sitting stiffly on one of those tiny red chairs slightly hollowed to take small bottoms, I had an accident. As the warm liquid became cold, so my terror grew. Movement would become necessary at any moment. Mrs. Harrison clapped her hands and announced that we would now march with our chairs held over our heads. Wouldn't that be fun? I refused to budge. Mrs. H. cajoled, the class stared and giggled, sensing what was wrong. In total misery I got up, raised my chair over my head and felt the damp run into my curls.

A few days later Mrs. Harrison announced 'Tomorrow, children, I am going to take you on a journey to China!' I looked forward to this quite literally, expecting somehow to be transported to that distant land. When it turned out to be only a story set in China, even though told with all Mrs. Harrison's customary verve, I felt cheated.

School was a perilous place where you had to tread with caution, standing clear until a situation had declared itself, sensing your way. There was one dreadful boy, about two years older than I, who with that sure instinct that seriously damages the ideas of the innocence of childhood, sensed my vulnerability. He lived only a few houses away and so was difficult to evade. He had a precocious interest in sex that frightened and disgusted me. He would talk of the little Wilkie girls, evoking imaginary scenes of my being bathed with them hinting at private parts and erotic discoveries. He seized hold of me in a repellent way, so that kicking at his shins was the only means of self-defence.

His bullying took the form of getting his small gang to capture smaller boys, take them down into the school basement and there pile them into the two-foot space that had been left between the partition of the last lavatory and the wall. The feeling of helplessness as more and more small fry were thrust in, struggling for release, was my first experience of panic in the face of irresistible pressure. When in a sermon I dimly encountered the idea that evil could become incarnate, it wore the face of this boy.

The idea that bullies are cowards, so dangerous as a general rule, was true in this case. He delighted to abuse—from a distance—the four placid Chinese boys at the school, sons of laundry men or restaurateurs. Their leader, with a name we pronounced as Hum Chuey, was the organiser of a game they played among themselves. They took a number of their Chinese coins with square holes in the middle and cleverly attached to these shredded lavatory paper so that they made a kind of shuttlecock. This they would keep in the air by the action of one side of the foot, using short quick movements or sending it high in the air or passing it from one foot to the other, and around and across their circle, counting in unison in Chinese. One day, having become exasperated with mocking abuse from their tormentor they gave chase with threatening Chinese shouts. He fled for cover to a teacher.

Slater Street Public School was adjacent to Kent Street Public School attended by the older children. We all shared the same schoolyard and the same Principal. He intrigued me greatly, for having been told, by the knowing, that he wore a wig I took every opportunity of inspecting the cruelly sharp demarcation where hair ended and the red-neck skin began. There was a rumour that an enterprising boy had suddenly turned on a fan, unseating the wig, but that may have been a legend born of early silent film comedies. The Principal believed in bringing to justice those who misbehaved, but showed a curious ineptitude in this connection. A long strand of virginia creeper had been pulled from the limestone front of Kent Street School. The creeper was in its autumn splendour, in red and orange, making one wonder indeed why anyone would wish to damage it. Both schools were paraded and the head marched up and down in front of us holding the length of ravaged creeper. He was full of outrage and demanded that the culprit confess. On an increasingly frantic note he shouted, 'Does any child know who has done this?' Silence. Who was going to own up when it was plain that the head was without a clue? Who was going to act as an informer, with little reward and the certainty of terrible ostracism? We dimly sensed one essential rule of life; if you are in authority do not reveal its limitations.

Then there was the affair of the truant officer's hat. It was a black caracul, a wonderful tricorne affair and as such easily stolen and hidden. The school's really bad boy, seeing the hat left on a table outside the principal's office, simply took it. Partly this was pure mischief and partly it was revenge against the truant officer who had harrassed him more than once. The under-principal knew better than to parade the school. But there were frantic searchings before the hookey man left hatless. He continued so for some days afterward. Then, the mischievous eight year old thief simply replaced the hat where he had found it, becoming a school hero as we contemplated his nerve.

In contrast to what could happen in the twilight zones of the basement and the schoolyard, where teacher supervision was thinnest, inside the school was a place of order and security. We were lined up in the yard by classes to be marched into the school by Miss Smith, an elderly lady of great energy and a curiously jaundiced skin. We learned a good deal from her about correct behaviour both in the mass as a class and as individuals. Spitting was then regarded as an assertion of masculinity, expressing itself especially among the rougher boys. One such, having delivered a creditable gob onto the concrete in front of the school door one recess, was caught by Miss Smith in the act. As she bore down on him and began her lecture an appreciative little crowd soon gathered. By this time the heat of the sun was causing evaporation: as the whisp of vapour rose from its disgusting source Miss Smith spoke in frightening terms of the fearful germs borne by it, seeking to enter our noses and nostrils and consume our lungs. Tuberculosis was then a terrible scourge for which there was no real remedy. Miss Smith was however, perhaps paradoxically, insistent that in our exercises we should inflate our lungs to the full: somehow she conveyed the impression that if this were not done the bottom ends of these organs would from disuse wither and decay, with fatal results.

Miss Smith had the trick of passing her enthusiasms, however unlikely, to all her pupils—even the awkward ones. Her success with children was partly because she was a real participant, sliding about in her galoshes on the small school ice rink in the yard, refereeing hockey games. She regulated the play by clanging on the school handbell and she frequently admonished those boys who were early exponents of the poke-check and of butting the opposition into the boards. It was often she who would organise a party of boys to shovel snow from the rink. Her great triumph was the school gramophone. She had conceived the idea that we should be marched into school to the sound of martial music. Only a gramophone could provide this. But the money would have to be raised. So Miss Smith organised a paper drive. The kids brought their bundles of newspapers until the quota was triumphantly achieved, making a link between home and school, especially where parents entered into the spirit of the thing. The gramophone stood proudly on a chair while we all marched passed our well-earned possession.

Miss Smith had an even greater triumph over the Tokyo earthquake of September 1923. She told us that a fearful thing had happened to a strange and remote city as the earth had trembled, rocked and opened up, followed by a consuming fire that had devoured all in its path. She asked us to bring clothing and money to help the Japanese children. Remembering how fortunate we were in the comfort and plenty of Canada, there was a remarkable response as the homes of the children were ransacked for cast-off clothing.

Even Miss Smith however was shaken one terrible morning when our small school was rent by the screams of one of the girls. She had been carrying crochet needles in her hand while running downstairs, had fallen and run one of the hooked needles into her eye. Her shrieks froze both teachers and taught where they stood. Then I suppose shock must have set in and the child's cries receded behind the voices of the comforting teachers, waiting grey-faced for the doctor.

Miss Smith had an unrelated namesake, Mr. Smith, the Supervisor of Singing for the School Board. He went about from school to school encouraging the teaching of his subject and occasionally participating in it. The tonic-sol-fa system was then regarded as the best way of teaching us to read and write music. Our own teacher had done her best with these mysteries. Mr. Smith, a short man with a large tweed stomach, decided both to investigate our skills and demonstrate his own. 'Now, children', he said in his expansive way, 'I am going to sing you some notes, a tune, and I want you to write them down'. In his baritone voice he did a simple tune, perambulating the aisles peering at what we were recording. Having gained only a feeble grasp of tonic-sol-fa, and being terrified by the prowling Mr. Smith, I was in a fix. It would be fatal to write nothing. I wrote the incomprehensible symbols simply at random. Fate brought Mr. S. to my elbow. 'What have we here?', he boomed. He saw at once what had happened and decided to turn it to account. 'This', he said, 'is the tune heard by this boy'. He then sang my cacophonous notes to the cautious laughter of class-mates, but to my burning shame.

Writing was taught to us by the Palmer system, imported from the United States. It had certain basic rules which were relentlessly drummed into us, allowing no deviations of practice. The key was the notion of the 'freehand'—there was to be no cribbed action of the fingers, instead the whole hand should slide upon the wrist, the back of the hand being parallel with the paper such that an eraser could be carried on the wrist while writing. Only thus could the flow and rhythm of the Palmer method be achieved; only thus could a society be generated free of calligraphic idiosyncrasy so that all were on a par. Thus did Palmer stand for one liberal principal, that of equality, but deny another, that of individual expression. To free us from bad habits, there were exercises intended to limber up the action of arm and wrist. These soon became objects in themselves, our efforts being competitively selected to be hung in the classroom and shown at the annual school exhibition. First you practiced the linear action, moving up and down with a slight angling toward the right. Then you went round and round in ovals, making a long cylinder-like figure across the page. Then came alternations—half an inch of up and down, then swinging with ovals, then back to up and down. All this we did, of course, without question. Except for one boy. His spirit being not yet broken, he simply took his pencil and by swinging his arm on the axis of his elbow, covered his paper. On the other hand there was a certain kind of kid, not of the brightest, but strong on conformity, who excelled at Mr. Palmer's dreadful exercises.

One day, turning over the as yet unused pages of my writing book, I was struck by their freshness and beauty. There they lay free of smudge or of Palmer's atrocities or of set exercise sentences. I was indeed the first ever to see them. It had occurred to me not long before that the figure five was the most beautiful of all symbols either of numbers or the alphabet. It combined straight lines in its upper part, set at a provocative angle, with a splendid swinging curve which could be made to contain a smaller curve as its terminal. Moreover we had just graduated from pencil to pen and inkwell, inaugurating about a decade of the inky second finger. Looking at the blankness some seven or so pages further on from present use, I took my pen, and after the kind of preliminary swirl above the page of the kind my father made with his Swan pen, inscribed in the centre of the page a beautiful figure five, about one inch high. I knew at once that my immaculate five could mean trouble, for our books were inspected regularly. When the fateful day came our teacher stood in the aisle looking in puzzlement at the digit standing alone in the centre of the page. I felt she was about to tax me with my madness, but she did not do so. She studied the page for a long time, regarded me closely, considered, and passed on.

Smaller children have not had time to develop beaky or fleshy noses, and really buck-teeth are rare. But projecting ears are dreadfully obvious, as well as having been given in the 1920s a special new idiom of derision with the coming of the aeroplane with its fixed wings. My agonies over this were compounded by one terrible flap sticking out further than the other, provoking suggestions that in a high wind I would gyrate. There was one withering moment when, with me sitting in the middle of the class, the magic lantern was switched on, projecting my head in silhouette on the screen about twice life size. This caused general merriment. Agony over my ears did not however generate any sympathy in me for the Principal and his wig.

Across from Slater Street School there was a gas or petrol station, an early example of its kind. One morning a fire broke out in it. The alarmed word went round the school, we were dismissed and told very strictly to go home, for the gasoline tank might explode. Of course we joined the crowd attracted by the excitement. The pump wagon came drawn by its grey horses, pounding up the street, the gleaming brass bell being clanged by one of the firemen. The heroic figures now mounting the machine had been sitting in their braces in the sun only a few moments before. The fire reels were indeed a major attraction in our downtown lives, for we would follow them for many blocks to see them in action. The police remained distant figures for unlike the firemen they could produce no spectacular rush culminating in hectic action. But the police were important on the day that a rabid dog was loose on the streets. We were kept closely in school until late in the afternoon when the all clear finally came; the dog had been shot by the police.

Father's impractical side was revealed yet more starkly when it came to the school concert. Teachers of small children love putting on miniature pageants in which the children can dress up, giving everyone a sense of participation. I was to be one of a group of retainers, bearing halberds, to march in and protect the King. The boys thus detailed were to ask their fathers to make the necessary weapons. Father produced a miserable object with a piece of cardboard for a blade, flopping disconsolately at the end of what was clearly and painfully, a broomstick. But the generous-minded father of another boy had made two halberds—splendid objects that looked utterly real, resplendent in gold paint. Miss Smith gave me one of these, discreetly disposing of father's offering.

Little peep-shows were popular in my second year at Slater Street in 1922. You took a shoe box, and at one end of it set up a miniature panorama, you cut a peep hole at the other end, and illuminated the spectacle by cutting a square hole in the top of the box and pasting tissue paper over it, thus letting the light fall on your creation. You then demanded a marble for a peek, offering your 'marlie a peek' at this price. Mine was something of a triumph, using picture postcards of London together with lead soldiers, guardsmen on sentry duty. It is possible that this idea was father's.

Certainly I owed to him, in part at least, an early preoccupation with words and how to use them. I was congratulated on writing 'the thief was detected and arrested', admiring, I suppose, the use of two verbs in a single sentence. So could begin a feeling for words and word constructs, their power, their flexibility and their challenge. I could read aloud with ease, making it possible to indulge in that much prized achievement 'expression', and so could become the best oral performer in the class, called upon when the inspector or any other visitor was present. Mind you, Anastas Dascovitch, in spite of her exotic background, was a serious rival, having behind her all the fierce dedication of a non-English speaking family using their adopted language to succeed.

To this day the name of Sam evokes a distinctive odour, that of a butcher's shop: this olfactory trip mechanism was set deep in my mind by sitting next to a boy of that name. When Angus arrived fresh minted from Scotland the class was much amused by his burred 'r's, especially when one day he was required to recite aloud in class the 'memory work' set the previous day. He stood up and stoutly declaimed:

> Acr-rr-ross the narrow beach we flit
> One little sandpiper-rr-r and I,
> Gather-rr-ring driftwood bit by bit
> One little sandpiper-rr-r and I.

By this time my sense of vulnerability at being 'English' had been partly assuaged by the adoption of conformity. Angus was someone who was conspicuously a newcomer.

By virtue of the family move we were now in the catchment area of Elgin Street Public School. It was necessary to become accustomed to a new ambience and a new set of teachers. The principal, Mr. McGregor Easson, was a distilled Scot. He sometimes took us for English lessons: there was the moment of near hysteria when he, his bald pate shining, read with magisterial deliberation lines from *The Burial of Moses*, including a reference to 'the bald old eagle'. He was one of nature's innocents. On one occasion, trying to explain to us what a piston was, he pumped the index finger of his right hand into the fist of his left. This caused much tittering from the more forward little boys. He had a tendency to fuss, accompanied by frequent denunciations of that failing: 'Don't fuss, boy', was a favourite phrase, inevitably earning him the nickname of 'Fusser'. But he took a real interest in his school and in his pupils. He was also formidable when this was necessary, so that even the most hardened boy could be deterred by the threat of being sent to the Principal.

The teaching methods at Elgin were a continuation of those at Slater. They combined the sense of discipline aiming at perfection, with the necessities involved in dealing with large numbers of children, both reinforced in varying degrees by a sense of sin. For the boys the Palmer System of handwriting was now joined by manual training classes. These also began from a kind of grammar, combined with the element of drill. Before you could think of making anything in wood you had to produce a plane surface and a plane edge, that is two near-perfect surfaces strictly at right-angles to one another as confirmed by the set-square. Only then did you proceed to your tie-rack or pipe-stand. This demand for 'true surfaces' had deep psychological roots in the minds of our educators, representing the notion of a foundation of order, together with that of character formation based upon its pursuit. Handwriting and manual training took their place alongside the learning of grammar, with its precise parsing of sentences. There was also 'learning by heart', through which long stretches of poetry were scored into our memories by sheer effort of will. This confidence in learning by rote the gems of our language took no account of the different capacities of children to remember, this being so bound up with what they knew, serving them as a system of mnemonics. Finally, there was, for our physical development, Swedish drill (though it was not called this), where the whole class (though boys and girls were separated for this) moved their limbs and bodies in unison to the calling of numbers by the teachers.

So it was that in Canada as in Scotland the permissive spirit of Rousseau elevating the notion of the spontaneous self-discovery of the child had been to a considerable degree repudiated. There was no simple sense that the child should exfoliate, drawing on inner riches, undefiled by the crass and tainted perceptions of grown-ups. Rather the adults were there to convey the established values and the testing skills of adulthood. But many of the teachers, especially the women, had an intuitive knowledge of what young children needed, and of the necessity to touch the springs of their creativity. This gift, however, was expressed in a brisk and unsentimental manner, within the overall presumption of adult control.

It is easy to patronise the Province of Ontario's system of education as practiced in the didactic and disciplined age of the 1920s and 1930s. It did no harm to the middling and bright children. If you made the necessary concession of conformity, you could then move on beyond Palmer to writing meaningful things, beyond the true surfaces and tie-racks of manual training to something in which you could take pride (perhaps even getting to use the school lathe), beyond grammar and memory work to a sense of structure, of images and writings sinking deep into the mind, and beyond collective drill to a sense of movement and co-ordination. If you were less bright, or perhaps if you were superlatively bright, you might find some of these various apprenticeships something of a nuisance, but no more than that. In general there was a basic reassurance in the thought that our teachers knew what should be done and would see to it that we did it.

The schoolyard saw many fights and skirmishes, but they were usually passing affairs, flareups that were quickly settled by the retreat of one contestant or the ringing of the school bell. But there was one epic battle at Elgin Street School that was bitter, prolonged and terrifying. One lad, Fred, had established himself as the fighter of the schoolyard, to whom all boys learned to defer. There arrived one day an Italian immigrant lad, Alfredo, of short and powerful peasant build. Not knowing the prevailing convention, he somehow collided with our fighting school mate. An irreduceable situation arose. Fred had to assert his hegemony, but Alfredo refused it recognition. Word of what was afoot spread through the school. The fight was to take place after the teachers had gone home. Sometime about 4.30 it began. Fred had learned something of boxing, but his ascendancy rested upon a kind of ruthlessness. Alfredo had no skill, but a stoical courage and a strong body. He took blow after blow without retreating or adopting any kind of guard, moving steadily forward to get at his opponent. Fred was forced to give ground so that the fight wandered about the playground, its circle of boys moving with it. The excitement and enjoyment reached a crescendo. But then it began to subside, replaced by misgiving. The fight had become total, muting the crowd of boys who were beginning to wonder how it would end. Alfredo was bruised and battered about the face; Fred was still largely unmarked, but was showing increasing signs of fear of the indestructable opponent against whom nothing availed. And indeed Alfredo's killer instinct, more deep rooted and atavistic than Fred's, had been called up from the depths by the punishment he had taken. He had from the beginning not been bound by the niceties of the Queensberry Rules; he was now under a kind of berserk urge to destroy. This release of the implacable in an amiable and placid boy now under the killer instinct, had carried the affair far beyond the fun of a schoolyard fight, carrying us to the edge of the abyss. Only the arrival of Mr. Easson, informed perhaps by one of the neighbours of the school, saved Fred from annihilation. There was a vast surge of relief that authority had arrived, capable of recalling Alfredo to sanity and of saving Fred from the blind force he had unwittingly evoked.

Father had six starched collars, about two inches high, of board-like stiffness. On Friday nights the two that had become soiled during the week were taken to the Chinese laundry around the corner and two others collected ready for Sunday. The day came when father thought us old enough to undertake collar duty. Though we had been to the laundry with him, this was different. The place now seemed sinister in the extreme. The owner responded to our timorous entry by sliding back the panel in his glass partition and appearing in the aperture in a cloud of steam, looking desperately oriental. We proffered the bit of paper with mysterious Chinese characters; the expressionless head disappeared into the dimness beyond, where vague figures moved about under a yellow light. We had been told tales of fearful deeds done by such people when they were under the influence of opium, including kidnapping and other terrible crimes. I felt a terrible claustrophobia in the tiny vestibule, fearing to disappear forever from the world of home, school and church. To my immense relief the yellow face reappeared, now beaming, as the father of Hum Chuey, greeted two schoolfellows of his son.

Some weeks later, after a heavy fall of snow, having become positively jaunty about the Chinese laundry, we met on our way home with the collar quota, one of the rougher boys who for some reason had become friendly. He was soon joined by two or three other boys allowed, unlike us, the freedom of the streets. The suggestion was made that we all go up the back alley and 'razz the Chinks'. Finding it impossible to extricate ourselves and being unwilling to show how family-bound we were, we went along. The party climbed up on the wall at the back of the laundry and when all were settled began shouting and barracking:

Ching-ching Chinaman
Sitting on a fence
Trying to pick a dollar
Out of fifteen cents.

For a long time nothing happened, while Eddie and I grew more and more nervous as the dark drew in, he clutching the collars and hoping they would escape the attention of our fellows. Suddenly the back door opened and Mr. Chuey and his family rushed out, no longer amiable, but shouting a terrifying mixture of English and Chinese. We all dropped off the wall into the alleyway. Being the smallest my short legs stuck in the deep snow while the rest ran away. I was lost in tears when Eddie crept back to pull me out.

CHAPTER 4

Britannia on the Bay

The signal that summer had really begun and that we were off to Britannia was the arrival at the door of Mr. Bagg and his truck. On a late May or early June day our modest load of furniture would be piled where the sawdusty ice had been in the morning. Eddie and I, after many injunctions to be careful, would climb up choosing comfortable chairs and loll as we rattled and swayed the seven miles. On the second such occasion our triumphal arrival at Britannia was sadly dimmed. Eddie, to make himself more comfortable, moved the cage of mother's canary. Instead of lifting it with a steadying hand beneath its bottom because of the weakness of its catch, he seized the top, the bottom fell away and mother's friend fluttered into the air above the Richmond Road and disappeared. How were we to tell her?

The village of Britannia-on-the-Bay, some seven miles from Ottawa, represented our escape from the fierce summer heat of the city, together with the attraction of village life and the access it gave to what was then the borderline between the confines of the city and the openness of land and river. It stood on Lake Deschenes, in fact on a widening of the Ottawa River. It had its own all-season residents, its continuous backbone, a few going back to the pioneer days. On them we refugees from the humid and torrid Ottawa summers imposed ourselves. This had become possible when the streetcars of the Ottawa Electric Railway Company, followed by the automobile, had made the seven mile journey easy.

The Ottawa Electric Railway Company's streetcar tracks and the Canadian National railway line ran parallel, about 50 feet apart, through Britannia, the former with its terminus about 200 yards farther on at the Britannia Park. The streetcar drivers, free of the city's traffic, would often open up their ponderous vehicles to full stretch when they reached the mile or so of open track between the fields as they approached the village, causing an exhilerating swaying and bucking as strong draughts of air were forced through the windows. A C.N.R. train passing at speed over the level crossing was terrifying with its rising paralysing roar and its rush of air trying to drag you into itself. One small child was indeed sucked in by this behemoth,

4   Children at Britannia, 1923. Note the distinctive Chevrolet badge on the radiator of the car. Edward sits on the front fender, Sydney on the front mudguard.

leaving almost no remains for the funeral. At a distance the lonesome whistle of the train made it sound a friendly thing, but close up at the crossing it was a monster terrifying with its noise and rushing wind.

The fares charged by the Ottawa Electric Railway were a source of concern and interest among the less affluent commuters to the city like ourselves. Some of those who had cars gave lifts; those who did not sometimes made 'arrangements' to occupy and pay for empty seats. This raised the dark question as to whether the tram car franchise was such that the company could prosecute car owners who thus carried for hire. This dire possibility was never tested.

Britannia was not a place for Ottawa's elite, but for those, like us, of modest means. The seasonal migration from city to village and back again was the governing tempo of our year. The village was to be our gateway to nature through the majestic Ottawa River, La Grande Rivière du Nord. So it was that downtown Ottawa with its contending inheritances from Britain and France and its borrowings from the United States, together with the village of Britannia and the Ottawa River, provided the setting within which, under our immigrant English parents' eyes, we went through our rites of passage as Canadians.

But even before the move we would visit Britannia by street car in the early spring when some of the snow and ice was still about. The air from the lake cut deliciously into our lungs so long accustomed to the central heating in the town. The lumberjacks would sometimes appear on the lake at this time, gathering up stray logs, and occasionally coming in strength to recover hundreds of them when a boom intended to be opened at the head of the Deschenes rapids had prematurely broken. We had heard of the heroes among them who could identify the key log in a jam, set it free and then race across the heaving and rolling mass to safety. They were sweaty, unshaven men in heavy spiked boots, with braces over coarse shirts, wet to the waist, wielding their peavies and pikepoles with great skill. They had curiously shaped boats, with points at each end, which they rowed not by the sweeping motion of a college crew, but by a short and choppy action. The ancient paddle wheeler, the *G.B. Greene*, once a pleasure steamer, still plied on the river, powered by the rocking arm of its beam engine, towing its boom of logs.

The only two 'public' buildings in the place, apart from the churches, were the two stores, one on each side of the tracks. Between them there was a keen rivalry for business, focussed upon the possession of the Post Office. Nasset's store was in the ascendant during the 1920s, but in the 1930s Tyrrell's gained ground, with the Post Office changing hands. This decline of fortune began when Mr. Nasset, augmenting his shop activities by acting as a part-time constable, was convicted of accepting some sort of bribe and so served a six months jail sentence, becoming the only person we knew who had a criminal record. The confidence of this large man who had presided over the nerve-centre of the village faded with his disgrace and his store became a shadow of its former self. Mr. Tyrrell whose star reciprocally rose, was a small but amiable man; his wife was very like him, but had some kind of hormone imbalance that made it necesary for her to shave about once a week. As children we monitored her beard with interest. Apart from the question whether one's family favoured Nasset's store or Tyrrell's, there was the matter of patronage as between the Ottawa Dairy or Producers Dairy, Standard Bread versus Morrison and Lamothe, or whether the family subcribed to the *Citizen* or the *Journal*.

Whichever store held the Post Office, collecting the mail was a source of some embarrassment for us as children. This arose because those families prepared to pay a modest fee had a key to one of the nest of mail boxes and so could get their letters without having to ask. Father believed that the service should be free and so refused to subscribe; there was too the fact that we had little money. This meant we had to ask whoever was on duty at the store to search through A to D to see if there was anything for us.

Our first summer home was in the New Mill, a kind of tenement owned by Mr. Tomieson, one of the few remaining pioneers of the district. He was in his nineties, and wandered about with a fruit basket full of rusty nails, providing what seemed to be the only maintenance service on his estate. His New Mill, together with its more ancient counterpart, the Old Mill, were supplied with water from Mr. Tomieson's own barrel-shaped water tank standing on its high rusty frame, leaking copiously, keeping the creaking windmill pump that surmounted it constantly busy.

Nearby there were patches of swamp where bullrushes of the kind that had sheltered Moses grew. Their stalks when tipped with nails made splendid arrows. Frogs, both large and small, with their seasonal croakings and mysterious frog-spawn—like sago pudding—lived there too. There were the fireflies, the irises (the 'flags') and the morning glories. The sharp-edged leaves of the swamp grasses would cut you between the toes if you were not careful. The great attraction of the woods was the birch trees, from which we cut small sheets of bark. Most of the trees were tall and straight, especially the pines—there were no gnarled oaks as on an English village green and no twisted shapes as in forest-haunted German fairy tales. Even so, we sensed the mystery of the woods and how Hansel and Gretel must have felt when lost in them. A garter snake, dark green with yellow stripes, slithering through the grass, was an unaccountable thrill.

The birds were full of life, so different from the dusty stuffed examples brought into class by a conscientious teacher, brilliant in colour and flashing and graceful in their movements—flickers, red-winged blackbirds, orioles, bronzed grackles, kingfishers, swallows and robins that mother told us were really thrushes (only England and Scotland had true robins, tiny sprightly creatures). The cry of the loon and the rushing wings and distended necks of the Canada geese in their great 'V' shaped skeins spoke of wild and distant places.

5   Britannia, 1923. Mother with the three boys. Kenneth was born in 1922.

As the same down-to-earth teacher pointed out to us, there were the insects, the necessary food for many birds. The mosquitoes were the most troublesome, though as children we were true Canadians in the sense of acquiring an early immunity to their bites that our parents were never to enjoy. The horseflies though less numerous were terrible stingers when you were wet from swimming, as well as carrying an aura of the unclean. Under certain summer conditions the shadflies would breed explosively and attracted by lights would cover screens and verandahs, leaving their soft-brown bodies to be swept up in heaps in the morning. Plagues of caterpillars might weave their dense webs over shrubs and the branches of trees. Water snakes and bats, though harmless, were treated as obscenities. Fishing worms were the object of our happy digging in the manure pile of Mr. Bagg, pulling the overfed creatures from their dungy heaven.

One family were neighbours of ours in the New Mill. Their daughter, of my own age, gave me my first fleeting introduction to the female psyche and anatomy, and their relationships. She showed a positive and persistent interest in matters that were at most of passing concern to me. When we were six or so she proposed a reciprocal showing of private parts, together with them performing, in their respective ways, the only functions we could as yet assign to them. I agreed, not quite knowing why. We adjourned under the verandah of the New Mill (the floor was placed high because of the spring floods). There the mutual demonstration took place, with a certain feeling on my part that there was nothing much to get excited about.

Still, she was a pretty little girl with her fair hair cut in a fringe. Her sense of adventure was in a way attractive, though it carried a vague sense of danger arising from the certain knowledge of stern parental disapproval if all were known. Not long after the anatomical exchange she had another proposal. The tenants of the New Mill were served by a set of numbered earth closets, two rows of five or so of such, back to back. Those of our two families were opposite to one another. She suggested that we should occupy our family compartments, and when she knocked on the partition, should shove our heads through the seats with a view to discovering whether we could see one another. This manoeuvre we carried out. Sure enough there was her disembodied head, with her innocent face, upside down, her hair clear of her face as though it were standing on end. We both became so enchanted with the sight thus afforded, ignoring the fearful mess below us, that we began exchanging loud greetings. Word must have reached her mother of strange doings, for there was suddenly a terrifying banging and her mother's voice shrieking, 'what is going on in there?' I never heard how this challenge was dealt with, nor did I worry, knowing that her ingenuity would see her clear of trouble.

There were some rough boys at Britannia. They had their own perverted sense of entertainment. One day we came upon them at a little patch of swamp. They had captured a number of green frogs and were doing terrible things to them. They had gathered fine hollow reeds and were thrusting these up the anus of each frog in turn, blowing them up and throwing the inflated creatures onto the water of the swamp with great amusement. These kids frightened us, seeming to be the negation of all that home and Sunday School stood for. There were, on the other hand another set of tough boys, with whom we had no problems. They were the nephews of a man with whom father had served in France. Father used to tell us that Nobby on going up into the line had said that he knew he was going to be killed. And so he was. There were always cordial greetings between father and this family. No doubt these boys had been told of the connection.

In late May the lake was gripping cold for the first swim. It was erratic in its flood behaviour, so that every spring brought the exciting question, how high would the flood waters rise? Almost every year they would surround low-lying cottages, so that one of the first jobs when the water level fell was to stand the privies upright again. The lake, being broad and shallow, could quickly become covered with whitecaps. There were several drownings each year, drawing us in morbid fascination to the end of Britannia pier, half hoping and half fearing to see the corpse of the missing boy or young man, bloated and inert, brought to the surface by the grappling irons of the Provincial Police. When, especially on a Sunday afternoon, a crowd of people began to move along the pier to its farthest end, we knew that someone had drowned. This would bring father hotfoot; in pursuit of the 'story' for the *Citizen*.

Edward and I were provided with cotton bathing suits gratefully received from a neighbour whose boys had outgrown them. They were horrid affairs which never seemed to dry. Mine was so large that the neck opening showed much of my rib cage and my tiny private parts were outlined as the damp cotton clung to them, the modesty shirt hanging over my knees.

Across the lake swept the great electric storms that ended spells of suffocating weather. We delighted in them, but they made our parents deeply uneasy, though they tried not to show it. The oppressive heat combined with a heavy dark sky caused us to stay close to home or go to the house of a friend. Then a curtain of rain would appear on the far side of the lake, advancing quickly. Then there would be a darkening of the sky as the downpour moved toward us across the water amid a general expectancy heightened by lightning and thunder. Then came the rushing wind bowing the trees before it. At last the searing flashes and roars and rumbles of limitless power were overhead, reminding you of God. As the storm passed the pelting rain would continue, heavy enough to flatten the waves. We would dash out in mild hysteria to swim in the downpour.

Across the lake, too, in midsummer came the splendid sunsets over Aylmer Point. Father took a special delight in these, sitting with mother on a log on the shore placidly drinking in the changing colours and musing on the manifestations of God and on the fate (God's will?) that had brought them there. The Milky Way and the few constellations he could identify reminded him of the Lord's infinity, though to dwell too much on the fathomlessness of space disturbed him. There were the 'Northern Lights' which lit the sky in late autumn with a dazzling beauty giving another, though rare, display of the Almighty's gift of colour. Their cold flashing brilliance was so different from the warm benediction of sunset. The trees in autumn, especially the maples, enthralled him. When the Canada geese passed overhead, with their outstretched necks and white under-sided wings, whooshing and calling, seeking the southlands before the lakes were locked in ice, we would all rush out, with father at our head.

In the distance stood Five Mile Island with its tiny white lighthouse, catching the sun. Very early it became one of our ambitions to reach it. There the Algonquin Indians had, we were told, buried their dead. All that remained of the race who had once possessed our river was Indian Joe, a local half-breed who was treated with fear by children and their mothers, and as an idiot by self-confident and aggressive men. This battered relic of the noble redman with his shaggy, greasy black locks wandered about wearing a mixture of cast-off garments, muttering unpredictably. He was alas no fit relic of his race, for whom land, air and waters were alive with spiritual forces. We did not really connect him with the noble figures we saw in old drawings and paintings, for the redmen who had built their lives around our river were long gone, with nothing of theirs to be seen except in the sad artifacts under glass in the Victoria Memorial Museum.

The deep timelessness of childhood summers settled in somewhere between the exhileration of the ending of school in June and the approach of the prospect of its return in September. Occasionally we would call in at our city home in high summer to find it filled with the stillness of suspended time, a light dust over familiar objects as they stood about, reproachfully waiting to re-enter our lives.

The Deschenes rapids were very dangerous, with a strong current ready to swallow any unwary craft that approached too close. The turmoil bristled with rocks on which logs had become stranded, piled and unpended by the power of the rushing water. A family friend had once had to row steadily for half an hour, watched by a crowd on the shore, in order to get clear: this became a cautionary legend. It was an injunction from father whenever he saw us in the rowboat, 'Stay away from the rapids'.

The falls had a further fascination, hinting at great ideas that had failed. Since the early nineteenth century there had been schemes for a Georgian Bay water route to the Great Lakes, making it possible for steamships to follow the Indian and voyageur route to the heart of

Canada without having to share the St. Lawrence system with the Americans. Nothing had come of such schemes. Work had begun about 1910 to build a canal to circumvent the Deschenes Rapids. But this, the last of such projects, had fallen through, leaving a cutting and embankments, together with a shelf at their upper end over which there flowed in the spring a considerable waterfall. There were various relics lying about including narrow guage rail lines and an old steam engine boiler. Deep grass, tamarack and fern, and in the late summer goldenrod and ox-eyed daisies hid much of this, adding to the mystery.

CHAPTER 5

Our Formal Introduction to God

Church made its demands in all seasons. In the winter we attended First Baptist Church at the corner of Laurier and Elgin. By this time it was no longer the 'Baptist Tabernacle', as was carved high up on its front, but a highly respectable, not to say comfortably bourgeois place. In England father had been a dedicated member of the Churches of Christ, also known as the Disciples of Christ, a strict and severe sect which was Baptist in origin. Its members believed not only in adult baptism by total immersion as the only fitting introduction to membership of the church, they also rejected totally the idea of a paid minister, insisting on the ministry of all believers. The Disciples were highly reserved about the higher criticism of the Bible that had come from Germany and which, as the cutting edge of a new liberal theology, was questioning the literal interpretation of the scriptures. Whereas father's father, a small scale Birmingham grocer, and three of his sons, also in the grocery trade, had been conformist members of the established Church of England, his mother had carried him, his three sisters and his brother James into the Disciples, into strong, not to say fierce, nonconformity. Their earnest evangelicalism had had a profound effect upon father; on his marriage certificate he had described himself as 'evangelist'. He felt himself to be in the tradition of John Bunyan. The puritanism of the seventeenth century and the uncompromising set of notions on which it was based had taken a powerful grip on him. These ideas included an abhorrence of the Roman Catholic Church and its dubious offspring, the Church of England. The search for the heroes of the Old Testament and for Christ had carried him to Egypt and the Holy Land, consuming the modest savings he had intended for his earlier abortive marriage. He took pride in the fact that President Garfield of the United States had been carried from log cabin to White House on his Disciple's faith, and that the fatherless Lloyd George had been raised as a Disciple by his uncle Richard, an Old Testament cobbler, a prophetic figure, emanating primitive goodness from his Welsh fastness. In Ottawa, however, there was no congregation of Disciples, leaving nearby First Baptist Church with its downtown setting as the next best thing.

6   First Baptist Church, Ottawa, Canada, *c.* 1935.

Our formal religious education had begun about the time I was six and our younger brother Kenny was born. We had come to the attention of the lady who so assiduously ran the League of Worshipping Children at First Baptist Church. We maintained a resistance for several weeks, but she, aided by our parents, finally overbore us, conveying us on the first occasion to the church in her car, a treacherous treat. The League sat in special pews at the front of the church for the first twenty minutes of the morning service and then withdrew to a room upstairs where we were regaled with Bible stories, children's hymns and prayers. It was, I suppose, a kind of crèche intended to make it possible for young mothers to attend church, as well as serving as a recruiting ground for the Sunday School.

We heard much of foreign mission stations with queer names. there was a great deal of talk of benighted peoples in Africa, India and Asia living 'in darkness'. We were asked to bring coloured pictures cut from magazines, old Christmas cards and picture post cards to be sent in bulk to them. We imagined that our offerings brightened up the interiors of mud huts. One mission in India was called something that sounded like Wee-ur-u, with very extended vowels. When we had gone to bed a few days after hearing a lady missionary holding forth with great earnestness about this place, Eddie in the midst of a giggling session proposed a farting competition. He then produced a masterpiece that sounded exactly like the lady's meticulous pronunciation. This reduced us both to hysteria, but this had to be controlled, otherwise father would come in his nightshirt to see what was going on.

In the summer at the cottage at Britannia we climbed the long hill out of the village up to the corner of the Richmond Road where stood the white wooden Presbyterian church (later United Church of Canada). It was a friendly place, a kind of epitome of summer, with birds, butterflies and bees sometimes at the windows to distract us. There were city types like ourselves, but there were also rubicund farmers, one or two of whom still left their horses and buggies in the stabling adjacent. The church had been built by the early Ottawa Valley pioneers, many of them Scots. It was simple to the point of starkness, painted white inside as well as out, as befitted an inheritance of John Knox. The pews were heavily coated with a varnish that became treacly in the summer heat so that your trouser's, especially if the sermon was a long one, could be bonded to the seat. When the congregation at last rose for the final hymn there would be a concerted rending sound as fabric and pine parted company. The adults pretended not to hear, but it made my brother and I giggle.

Mother did not attend church in the mornings in winter or summer. Preparing dinner was her priority. But she sometimes went with father to evening service in winter at First Baptist, the two of them clinging together as they slipped along on the Ottawa ice. Mother had been raised a Wesleyan Methodist in Bristol, and had been much attached to her Chapel there. Indeed she was never quite at ease; she felt she had deserted the religion of her childhood and upbringing. She took no part in church suppers, missionary suppers or the like at First Baptist. To have done so would have brought her into the circle of middle class Canadian ladies. She preferred to spend her evenings reading. Perhaps she felt that our home was not such that she could return the hospitality of the wives of comfortably placed men. Also we three boys must have been a heavy drain on her energies, making her glad to close her day with rest.

The minister of First Baptist when we first knew it in the early 1920s was the Reverend Dr. Maplin. We learned to regard him as leading a kind of double life. When he came to the Sunday School all was sweetness and light, concerned with the innocence of childhood and with youth and its golden potential. But we were to learn by the time that we were eight that there was another side of mankind where the darkness of sin ruled. For some preachers still, including Dr. Maplin, Hell was a real and indeed lively prospect, mysteriously but inescapably linked, as it was to come to seem to us, with sex, with the implication that the fire of the one was the price you paid for indulging in the other. Dr. Maplin, once warmed to the prospects of damnation, did not mince words, but dilated on the terrors of the pit with its fire and brimstone. The older evangelicalism could work powerfully in him, especially when at the evening service there was a higher level of suggestibility to the infernal shades. In such moments he could generate an enormous bull-roar of warning, accompanied by pulpit thumpings. On the relatively few occasions when he went the whole hog, calling for repentant sinners to declare themselves by coming forward to the front of the church, he would suddenly change his tone to quiet and confidential persuasion, urging us all to cast aside that very moment the burden of sin. This invitation to public exhibitionism generated in us a mixture of embarrassment and curiosity, both sensations being intensely felt. As Dad preferred to sit fairly close to the front of the church we could not see what response there might be behind us, causing a powerful temptation to turn and look, arrested only by Dad's grasping each of us by the thigh. No one when we were there ever did respond. First Baptist Church had by the early and mid-twenties left open penitence behind. We used to wonder what these nameless sins might be to warrant such dire warnings; it seemed to us it would be more inducive of good behaviour if the minister were to be more specific.

That Dad should thus restrain us was fully in character. For though he condemned out of hand the ritualism of the Roman Catholic and the higher Anglican churches, he had a high sense of decorum. Loud were his condemnations at meetings of the deacons and elsewhere of a minister who failed to do things, as he put it, 'decently and in order'. When the pulpit fell vacant after retiral a hopeful young candidate, having got through the morning service with credit, presided over the communion table. The wine (non alcoholic of course) was served in the individual glasses (tiny but very thick and squat), typical of Baptist

Churches, arranged in round cruets with clear varnished wooden covers. A pair of these was placed at each end of the table; between them were four plates on which were heaps of cubes of white bread resting on fine lace made by the ladies of the church. The whole was covered with a starched very stiff linen sheet of brilliant whiteness. The ladies responsible for the cloth had, as usual, ironed it so strongly into its folds that Dr. Maplin with a few quick but deliberate movements like a magician could have reduced it to a tight parcel which he placed on a bench behind him. But for the young visitor who hoped to become our new minister the cloth was to be his downfall. In his nervousness he jerked it from the table, looked at its intransigeant starchiness in a panicky fashion, failed to find its folds, crushed it into a shapeless bundle and thrust it under the table. To our fascinated eyes it lay there, desecrated, stirring slightly like a living thing as the rigidities worked into it by the ladies struggled against the disgraceful disorder imposed on it by the unhappy visitor. As Dad squirmed beside us in the pew we could feel his outrage.

One evening father's sense of decorum was placed in conflict with his fear of calamity. Just as the sermon was about to begin I whispered that I needed to go to the toilet. The slightest threat that we might wet ourselves we knew would bring a galvanic response at whatever cost of inconvenience or conspicuousness. Palpably annoyed at the lack of forward planning on my part, but apologetically bent, he led me the length of the aisle while the minister waited. Having visited the basement there was the problem of what to do next. The minister could not be interrupted again by a return parade up the aisle. We had therefore to stay in the vestibule. But it was a cold winter night. Some old farmer had left his vast coon coat in the vestibule. Dad, having wrapped me in this, opened the door to the church slightly so that he could satisfy his inveterate taste for sermons. So I sat in an odorous heap of fur, badly cured and nauseously impregnated, while the voice of the preacher came faintly past father's engrossed form.

This experience did not however put me off. By the age of eight occasional attendances at evening service had a certain charm. There was a brightness and a cosiness in the church of a winter evening when people seemed closer to one another and to God, perhaps indeed also to the fear of Hell. On one such evening a bat somehow abandoned the inside of the spire where dust and cobwebs had been gathering since 1877, the year in which the church was built. It made its way into the church itself and began to range to and fro. It swooped lower and lower as the congregation wavered uncertainly through the closing hymn, trying to be staunch and steady, but waving like a field of wheat as the bat swooped by. Some panicky deacon sent for the

7   The Checkland boys and their mother in Ottawa, 1926. Note the knicker-
bocker suits lovingly made by their mother.

janitor. This ancient took up a position standing on a pew at the back, swiping out with a broom. His zeal had no effect on the bat, but somehow reduced our sense of fortitude to bathos. The minister could, of course, observe the course of the bat in both directions, but as it never quite reached his end of the church he could still pronounce the benediction with slow and maddening deliberation.

The church on the hill at Britannia could also produce its mild drama. One summer Sunday we arrived just before the service was due to begin. The elders had gathered at the back and there was a buzz of consultation among them. Their patriarch walked down the aisle to where we were sitting. The Minister was missing. Would Dad begin the service? Somewhat flustered Dad put his straw hat (boater in England) on the sill of the open window. He soon rallied, moved to the pulpit and announced the first hymn. As the time for the sermon approached we could see him looking more and more anxiously at the back of the church. Just as we could feel him becoming desperate the Minister appeared and panted down the aisle. At this moment the window sash crashed down on the rim of Dad's hat. In his relief he heard nothing. After the service we rescued the hat and without warning presented it to Dad at the door of the church just as he was being thanked by the Minister and his elders. He put it on his head, whereupon the brim on the left side hinged down over his ear. The Minister was soothing, 'It will be all right if you iron it with damp brown paper'. On the walk home the guillotined brim fell off into the road.

The other three churches at Britannia were all small white clapboard buildings, scattered about the village. The Anglicans had as their vicar at St. Stephen's, the Reverend Lewis, whose wife was almost as prolific as Trollope's Mrs. Quiverful. He was something of a figure of fun, sometimes bathing off the end of the pier in an antideluvian costume that seemed to drape him almost as completely as his cassock, but which, because it was made of clinging cotton, revealed more of himself than he realised. Occasionally father would take us to Mr. Lewis's church 'for a change', and would enjoy himself seeing if he could find his way round the Book of Common Prayer. Mr. Lewis, surpliced and in command, reciting the litany of Laud, would shed his comical aspect and assume the full dignity of his calling. Some time in the late twenties a film company basing a film on Ralph Connor's Glengarry novels invaded Britannia. They made shots of the Anglican congregation, provoking among us excited identification of its members.

The Roman Catholic Church, that of St. Bonaventure, we never of course attended during the mass, but we did look in a few times. Because it was externally so simple and bright, so different from the dim splendours of the Basilica, it seemed not greatly different from the Anglican or even the United Church, suggesting some hope for a united Christendom. The priest we never saw. Behind his church was a woodland, known as Taylor's bush. It provided a dark pine backdrop against which the tiny white church stood out, a brightness against the dark, so different from Dad's view of Catholicism as being a thing of gloomy superstition. The film company shot scenes in Taylor's bush showing a man wrestling for his life with a bear.

The United Church on the hill where Dad's straw hat had been ravaged, was the nearest the village got to Calvin, Knox and Bunyan and the embracers of the reformed faith that had rent northern Europe in the sixteenth and seventeenth centuries. In our everyday lives as neighbours in the village these ancient differences had no place— people simply accepted religious preference as given and immutable. But the maintenance of the distinctions was, at another level, real. The long struggle to create the United Church of Canada, which was finally successful in 1925, though leaving dissenting fragments, was evidence of how men will divide on what must be, even to an omniscient God, pretty fine print if ancestral loyalties are involved. An older schoolmaster shocked me by remarking quite casually that we all held the religion we did because we got it from our parents: so much for what was sometimes said or implied from so many diverse pulpits that there was only one truth and that God would cause it eventually to prevail over all others. As good Baptists, when we reached the English Civil War at school (we learnt history in Canada as if we were English), we knew we were Roundheads, opposed to the frivolities of the Cavaliers, though we didn't much like all that stuff about being killjoys.

CHAPTER 6

Summer Village Life

When I was approaching the age of eight father, with mother's con-currence, decided, after much anxious cogitation and consideration of the financial position, that the time had come to build our own cottage. Once he had overcome his misgivings, Dad entered into this adventure with zest. He employed an immigré Englishman to do the building. The plans were simple, for we could not afford much—a living room, a kitchen and two bedrooms, but they were pored over long into the night. He wanted some little reminiscence of the Old Country: the result was some laths around the top of the living room walls to simulate the half-timbering of Shakespeare's England, and a 'fireplace' for which we could not afford a chimney and so it housed a somewhat ineffectual electric fire with illuminated 'coals'. Nor could we afford to build a cess pit: there was nothing for it but a tiny hut, complete with a sanitising carton of lime, at the bottom of the lot. This was reached by walking along three heavy planks.

The site was low-lying and so the cottage had to stand some four feet above the ground as a precaution against floods. A mistake was made in placing the house. It was as much as seven feet into the adjacent lot; father lived in dread our neighbour would discover this. But it pleased Eddie and me to be that close to the next cottage because it housed two attractive girls who could, with care, be observed to advantage from our adjacent windows, an amenity which was begin-ning to have its attractions and which improved with time.

At the cottage tap water came from the river and so was thought unfit to drink. This was especially so during those summers in which there was a polio scare. It was one of our jobs to carry water from Mr. Train's pump about one-quarter of a mile away. We did not really have proper permission for this because Mr. Train feared his well might be exhausted. It was necessary to pump slowly in order to minimise the squeak of the handle as it brought water up from the depths, cold and clear, but with a noticeable taste of iron. Another boyhood task was to carry the ice in from the back doorstep to the ice-box, having first flushed the sawdust from it with a pan of water. Ice, cut earlier

8   Clifton Cottage, Britannia, showing the Union Jack, *c.* 1927.

in the season from the lake, and stored in a cold house, was delivered at dawn by the taciturn Mr. Bagg.

Father revelled in the building of the cottage and rejoiced in its successful completion. It inspired him to do uncharacteristic things. He himself put up a set of simple shelves for the kitchen, as well as affixing a hand-painted sign 'Clifton Cottage' to celebrate mother's Bristol birthplace. Finally he bought a Union Jack and hung it in triumph from a pole at the corner of the verandah.

At Britannia we made friends in a way that was impossible in the city. Of these Jon Flynn was, for me, the closest. He was a Roman Catholic of Irish extraction, with uncles and aunts and cousins who were of farming stock near Prescott. It was Jon who widened my horizons. He introduced me to the use of the axe and he proposed projects. We could build a raft for the river. We could attempt a signalling system over the fifty yards between our houses by means of a length of string—unfortunately the stretch in the string was so great that tugging at one end sent no signal to the other. It was he who proposed that we should offer ice-cold lemonade for sale for five cents a glass. Jon had learned from his farming relations how animals were bred, though he had to admit that when he and his cousin tried to fathom the secret of a bull's virility by opening up a testicle they had somehow acquired they were defeated. Even the desperate expedient of trying to crush it in a vice failed.

Jon lived with his parents and two aunts in 'Dombey Hall', a two-storey frame house facing the lake. No one knew what had inspired the former owner to name the house in such a Dickensian fashion. It had a hipped roof, painted green, with white pillar posts and a verandah that went all the way round. In front of it stood an ancient willow with branches so close to the house that it had had to be lopped. In its crotch was a platform, the remains of a tree house nailed there by an earlier generation of kids. The living room of Dombey Hall contained a large fireplace built of boulders, across the top of this there was a series of improving mottos and quotations set in tiny frames including 'If a man can build a better mousetrap than his neighbour the world will beat a path to his door'. There was an old grand piano on which the occasional visitor would play popular songs. Even more ancient was an Edison phonograph with its vast horn and its cylindrical records, one of which rendered in a reedy tenor:

O'Brien
Is tryin'
to learn to talk Hawaiian

The party-line telephone was attached to the wall, making it possible to eavesdrop if one raised the receiver carefully and made no noise. At the back of the house was a hen-run, with an upturned derelict skiff as shelter for the hens.

Jon's family was a devoutly Catholic matriarchy. His father, a subdued man of great girth who struggled to keep a small grocery store in Ottawa afloat amid low incomes and bad debts, died when Jon and I were about eight. Mrs. Flynn was one of the five Cooney sisters who were the unifying force of the family. She was uneasy that there might be quarrels among us boys over religion. Aunt Lena, in spite of her Catholic Irish heritage, was a fierce monarchist, revering George V second only to the Pope. The most vivacious of the sisters was Madame Frontenac who mixed in her children the Irish and the French inheritances. They were the most debonaire people we knew. I looked with great respect and intense curiosity at Mary Frontenac who had a vocation to become a nun. The farming branch of the Cooneys was presided over by another aunt and her husband, both looking weathered and worn, as sepia photos of early pioneers.

The Flynn-Cooney house became a kind of second home, in striking contrast to my own. Here Irish Catholic piety of an accepting, unquestioning kind ruled. Here too were deeper and broader Canadian roots, the product of several generations, not greatly interested in the misdeeds or misbeliefs of the world, and certainly not out to chastise or correct these. There were crucifixes, pictures of the Sacred Heart of Jesus, rosaries on dressing tables. When a storm threatened across the Lake Mrs. Flynn would light a votive candle and tell her rosary, invoking the piety derived from old Ireland against the fierce electric storms of the new world.

The adult who, apart from our parents, played the largest part in our lives, was Mr. Blewitt. He had been a contemporary of father's at the Wesleyan Day School in the heart of Birmingham: they had met in mutual astonishment in Spark Street, Ottawa, not long after my parents had arrived in Canada. Mrs. Blewitt had not been one of mother's closer wartime friends, for the Blewitts had settled in Britannia, spending winters and summers there. But it was through them that the Britannia connection had been made. Their son was a close friend, second only to Jon Flynn. Bill, lithe and blonde, could throw a stone farther and climb a tree higher than any of us, but he was little use with a ball.

Stanley Blewitt was a shortish man, but marvellously muscled. He had been a gymnastic champion in England. There was a studio photograph of him, heavily posed. His singlet, bulging with his splendid pectorals, was covered with medals, while one hand rested on a table bearing three cups and a shield. He fascinated us with his muscular control, being able to make biceps, pectoral and abdominal muscles jump at will. He had us giggling wildly as he passed the rhythm from one to the other as with the instruments of an orchestra, in time to his singing of

> *Tottie will you go,*
> *Tottie will you go,*
> *Down to the banks of the O-hi-o.*

He was a marvel with the Indian clubs, having drilled acres of young men in public demonstrations in the Old Country. He taught us some of the movements, which we mastered, though not before there had been collisions between heads and clubs. He believed in the development of the upper body, dismissing the spindly torsos of runners as inferior. He taught us the rudiments of boxing. He was a real ham, who loved to entertain, which he did marvellously well. On leaving Birmingham he had auctioned off his own furniture in the street to general acclaim. One dull winter Sunday at Britannia he dressed and made up as a woman, visiting various families, posing as having

mutual friends. He fooled everbody. The climax came when he produced one of the cigars of which he was so fond and as he lit it, watched
through the encircling smoke the dawning recognition.

He and his wife though still recognisably English, had assimilated
to Canada in a way our parents had not. They were part of the year-
round village community of Britannia. Stanley was a practical man,
teaching us to use the cross-cut saw, how to mix paints and how to
make cement; indeed he had a genius for rallying boys to help him
with his jobs so that they both enjoyed themselves and learned. He
was a do-it-yourself man rather than a craftsman, well adapted to his
penumbra of the Ontario frontier; one soon learned that finesse was
secondary to getting the jobs around the place done. This family had
pushed up the Ottawa River for thirty miles to Fitzroy Harbour, building a shack on an island just below the Chats Falls well before the dam
was built. It was there that we first really sensed the wilds of Canada.

During the war Mr. Blewitt had been a physical training instructor
for the army: indeed there was a group photograph with him domi-
nating the middle of the front row and our father with his much less
grand musculature on the back row. But Stanley never went overseas.
This, together with the fact that father was much better with a cricket
ball and a football, kept the balance of esteem between them. Stanley
combined his adaptation to the Canadian way of life with the role of
establishment conformist, for he was a member of the Church of
England, a Mason and voted Conservative. This could give rise to
careful fencing between him and father, as well as providing us with
two perspectives on how to respond to the world. Indeed Stanley
Blewitt was an alternative role model to father, a fact that father dimly
sensed.

Stanley's principal job was an unadventurous one as a civil servant
of modest rank. He also had a part-time one as physical instructor at
Ashbury College, 'The Eton of Canada'. From the college he brought
home used footballs, cricket bats and other sporting gear which provided the basis for our games. For some occasion or other at the College
he had built a miniature stage, about four feet across, in which he had
depicted historic scenes like the Battle of Waterloo. He had mounted
tiny cannon from which issued cigar smoke blown by him through a
tube to the accompaniment of booming noises made by his small boy
assistants. This marvel was shown to us with great pride. The effect of
fluted columns defining the procenium arch had been achieved by
gilded corrugated cardboard.

In those days there were 'war canoes' on Lake Deschenes. They
were racing craft with a crew of paddlers together with a helmsman
or cox. On quiet summer evenings we knew the young men of the

9   Cricket on the 'beach' at Britannia in front of Clifton Cottage; the Checkland boys and friend, Summer 1926.

Britannia Boating Club (the BBC) were practicing for a regatta, for we could hear across the water the shouted orders of the helmsman, together with his barked counting to set the stroke. One, two, three, four would reach us from the silhouetted shape, like a centipede on its back with its legs (the paddles) kicking in unison. As the sun lowered in the sky it flashed on the wet blades, making a rhythmic scintillation. The canoes were a kind of memory of the Indians of earlier generations, transmuted into a white man's competitive sport, participated in by young men who were mainly incarcerated in Ottawa offices on week-days and had to work off steam somehow. The competition among the boat clubs of the district was vigorous; the new Edinburgh Canoe Club crew used to sing

> *I'd rather be a horseball*
> *Than belong to the B.B.C.*

The larger animals had long since disappeared from Britannia, but one evening the older boys made a remarkable discovery down by the rapids in the old canal cutting. It was a turtle, nearly two feet across the shell. They bore it in triumph to the Old Mill, arriving just after

10   Are we playing cricket, football or baseball? The Checkland boys and
friends at Britannia, Summer 1928.

dark, with their trophy tied to a plank with a winding of rope. Parents
brought out flashlights to see what was going on. The beams revealed
the excited and triumphant faces of the captors as they crouched
around their prisoner, shouting their accounts of their adventure, the
difficulties of getting the turtle onto the plank and its weight over the
long walk. No one had ever seen such a thing. Everyone, including
parents, marvelled at the size of the captive, speculating on its origins
and where it had lived all those years. Someone told of the Iroquois'
myth of a giant turtle that carried the world on its back. The boys had
followed some sort of instinct in bringing it home. Slowly the hubbub
died down, leaving the question, only now able to surface, namely
what was to be done with the creature? It could hardly be released

among all those cottages, especially as someone suggested that it was a snapping turtle. There was nothing for it but to carry it back to where it had been found. When released it padded into the water of the cutting and disappeared into the darkness, a lone survivor of the creatures of the wild.

Not long after one of mother's friends from England paid us a visit. She was a shy but pleasant person, who earned her living as a companion for genteel ladies of comfortable means. It was her custom to go for a before-breakfast walk. On her second morning with us she returned badly shaken. She had been passing one of the electric cable poles when she noticed a curious shape at the top of one of them. It was an electrocuted linesman. He hung limp and livid from his safety belt in a curious 'n' shape. The poor lady visitor kept strict control while she went to the Post Office to report this terrible sight. In general she would have kept indelicate or violent things from children like us, but this morning she simply collapsed on a chair in the kitchen and her awful story poured out.

Most of the cottages were of wood and their pine clapboard and shingles made them highly inflammable. No summer went by without two or even more burning like torches. By the time the fire brigade arrived the furniture of the adjacent houses had been hurriedly carried out by the men and boys and lay in disarray in the yards and on the roads. There was debate as to how far the fire would spread. Much depended upon the prevailing wind and on the distances between cottages.

By the time you got to the scene the first house would probably be on the point of collapse. Its frame would stand starkly and briefly as the carpenters had first erected it, all else burnt away, like some mad firework display. The upward rush of air would carry fiery particles into the sky, a fearful demonstration of the principle of convection that our physics teacher at school tried hard to demonstrate to us with his candle and smoke in a box. The moment would come when the crowd would sense that collapse was near, when it came, all would brace themselves, then let out a kind of communal sigh. By now the next house would be well alight, starting with the roof of pine shingles. The firemen would concentrate their efforts on wetting the roof, but usually it was hopeless, unless there was a considerable gap between houses. So the consuming sequence went on. Men would rush into more houses, carrying out furniture and pictures at random, while the women folk hid their faces in their hands. Finally, the devastation would yield to a gap, or to the rallying of fire brigades from miles around. Water would be played on the charcoaled ruins until even the steaming had ceased. Then, especially if the fire had started at night, there would begin the search for the remains of those who had burned with their houses. The firemen would carry out mysterious tarpaulin-like bags. When this was done we children would wander among the ruins, marvelling at mis-shapen bottles and curved gramophone records, at stone or brick chimney pieces blackened and blistered but still standing, pointing out to each other views that could now be seen from new angles from among the devastation.

Such fires drew us, like drownings off the end of the pier, in spite of ourselves. Our parents made no attempt to restrain us, for such holocausts were a communal affair. But the sound of the fire engines terrified our small brother, setting him screaming. On most occasions he would follow Eddie and I about when he could, but when there was a cottage fire he sought refuge with mother.

It was Lake Deschenes and its parent the Ottawa River, La Grande Rivière du Nord of the *courier du bois*, that made it possible for us as older boys to withdraw from parents, teachers and preachers. It provided the essential elements of imagination, struggle, mild adventure and, was in effect, our rites of passage. By the same token it brought a feeling for the Canada of the Indians and of the early adventurers and settlers, of water that could be placidly still, rushing or storm-stirred, of fore-lands, wide bays, cliffs and crags, distant hills, pine forests and reeds bending with the wind. While we were on the river, home, school and church, so impregnated with the Old Country in its Victorian age, receded, along with pettifogging employment, allowing us to come to terms with ourselves in a Canadian setting.

First came the building of a raft. We were about eight years old; gathering a few logs of the right size and some boards was easy enough. Pinching a handful of six-inch nails from Mr. Blewitt's garage carried a frisson of risk, together with a twinge of Sunday School and sermon—inspired conscience. But these were lost in the joy of construction. Driving the great nails into the yielding pinelogs had its special satisfaction, being both an assertion of mastery and an act of creation. Then came the job of pushing the raft out into deeper water until it floated clear. Bill, Jon, Ed and I jumped aboard with poles or old paddles. The crowning achievement was to attach a wooden packing case, forming a cabin. This made the raft very tippy. All this was done with blissful concentration and anticipation.

But we had not reckoned with Mr. Blewitt. He did not reproach us over taking his nails. Instead he chose a more dramatic line. Did we realise that these logs belonged to the timber company? He pointed out the identifying marks on their larger ends which we had of course already noted. Did we not know that these logs would eventually go to the sawmill? At this point, as so often with Mr. Blewitt, histrionics

11   Britannia Bay, Summer 1925. The Checkland boys and friend in rowing
boat. The boom had burst and so the logs filled the Bay.

took over. At the mill the faithful attendant on the great circular saws
stood at his post while log after log slid up to its revolving teeth. Then
came one of ours, bearing our six inch nails. The good man could not
be expected to see them. There would be a blinding flash as the teeth
struck the nails, shattering themselves and slashing into the attendant.
How would we feel then? We were chastened: the joy had gone out of
the raft.

But there was one good outcome. Father had covertly noted our
rafting activities and had become worried that we might push out too
far from shore, be caught by a wind, be overtaken by a white-capped
storm or be swallowed up by the rapids. A flat-bottomed rowing boat
would be much safer. Accordingly, in the spring of 1924 he bought
us one, second hand, of course. On arrival it leaked badly, for it had
been standing out of the water for many months, its planks shrinking.
Dad undertook to caulk its gaping seams with oakum. It was some
time before he learned that what the boat really needed was to be half
filled with water and left to stand while the wood swelled, closing most
of the cracks. He then took great pleasure in painting the whole thing
a cool grey. This was the final stage of waiting. When the paint was

dry father and mother came down for the launching. Father's sense of occasion required that he and mother take the first ride. Neither had ever been on fresh water before except in a hired boat in an English park. Father took the oars and sedately rowed into the calm lake with mother sitting in the stern, giving a kind of benediction to the whole proceeding. As they moved along the shore we followed them, happy to see father trying to come to terms with the lake and mother enjoying one of her few sharings of our male world. At last they returned to the launching point and father armed mother ashore.

It was our turn. Ed seized one oar and I the other. Off we went in triumph with Jon and Bill and little Ken as passengers, staying, as instructed, close inshore. It was not long before the competitive urge for speed set in. With a rising tempo we tugged at our oars. In the excitement Ed's oar went down between two boulders, the boat moved

12   Sydney relaxing, Ottawa River, 1931.

relentlessly on, there was a terrible snapping sound and Ed's blade lost half its length. In this way our oars remained throughout the years of the row-boat, one with half a blade, a permanent reminder of the day of the launch.

Yet it was the row-boat that first gave us the freedom of the Lake, or at least our part of it. We saw beneath the waters the remains of old cribs built to anchor the booms in the old logging days, still mysteriously visible beneath the earthy yellow water of the Ottawa. With their frightening iron spikes projecting they had a Jules Verne kind of threat about them. As our daring increased we ventured farther out into the lake. The shoreline would redefine itself, as the group of cottages to which ours belonged receded and shrank, hinting that our places of security and intimacy were but a tiny part of the universe. At the same time landmarks not otherwise visible would rise up out of the landscape, especially the water tank at the Park, and the great chimney of the nickel works at the village of Deschenes, by the rapids.

We began our explorations of the shoreline around the southern side, away from the rapids. About two miles on we discovered what we called Clay Bay. Here for the first time we built a fire to cook our sausages and heat our beans. We soon learned that it was no good having a large and ravening fire: you needed concentrated heat and you needed to rest your frying pan, saucepan or kettle on something. This called for a small fire between rocks, with a good draught. This lesson meant that we inspected cowboy films with an expert eye to see whether the fire really could have cooked the meal and made the coffee. More than half the movie cowboy-cooks failed the test. But we soon learned to cheat a little—we found two railway sleeper spikes that served excellently as a support for pans when put across the fire. These we cherished as basic equipment.

On one of these trips Eddie was sitting at the back of the boat playing his mouth-organ. This he did with intense concentration. Bill was beside him wielding a paddle. He accidentally struck Ed's elbow so that the mouth-organ shot across his face through the air and into the lake. By the same continuous motion Eddie curved from his seat and into the water. But it was no good—the mouth-organ was gone. No more would father include in his imitation of what he called 'Wild Animals I have known' a mime of Eddie on the mouth-organ with elbows jerking to right and left.

But the row-boat was slow and heavy as it thumped its ponderous way along. A canoe was the thing. It was living and vibrant, responding to the waters that bore it, rising and falling, cutting the waves. Then there were paddles as opposed to oars—lighter and more shapely, entirely mobile in your hands, not as with oars tied to the craft and

13　Mr Bagg's Ice Trunk, used to carry canoes at start of longer canoe trip, Summer, 1935.

confined to a single arc. But canoes were deeply distrusted by father as being tippy and treacherous, only to be handled by experts. They were also expensive, at least in terms of our family resources. But salvation was at hand. Jon Flynn's family had a summer lodger, Dalton Macdonald, who owned a canoe but seldom used it, his courtship being largely conducted via his sports car. From occasional borrowings, cheerfully acceded to, Jon and I gradually took over the canoe when we were about thirteen. It was one of those gifts which, coming at the right time, meant so much.

With it our range of movement and intimacy with the lake expanded. We made our way to the raft from which the *G.B. Greene* released its logs. It was moored about a mile above the rapids, from which a boom descended downstream to guide the logs into the cauldron. By this time it was little used, but it was with a feeling of high adventure that we stepped out onto its planking.

The next, even more compulsive, objective was Five Mile, or Aylmer Island. It had long been part of our consciousness, standing out with different definitions depending on the weather and the light. When the sunshine was bright the tiny wooden lighthouse, a relic of the great logging days, would shine forth in brilliant whiteness. At night its modest light would twinkle across the lake. We had heard too that the

14 Setting off for a canoe trip. Edward and Sydney are on the right, 1935.

Island had been a burial ground of the Algonquin long ago. Five miles is a considerable paddle, especially across a wide expanse of water that could break into whitecaps within the hour. Stepping ashore on the Island carried the curious sensation that we were the first to do so. There is an abiding mystery about islands, especially small and empty ones far from the shore, a sense that you are in possession, but yet are an intruder who ought not to be in such a place. We explored every corner of our miniature but temporary kingdom and then swam from its beach. After lunch we lay on in the sun, but could not settle. The feeling of intrusion was strong. We were looking anxiously for changes in the weather lest the spirits of the air should punish us for our presumption.

One day Jon decided that paddling the canoe was a wasteful consumption of energy, and that what we needed was a sail. He produced an old tent whose canvas had partly rotted with which to make it. We felled a sapling for the mast. Fortunately someone else had had the same idea and had fitted a board in the bow which made stepping the mast easy. A second sapling served as the boom. So it was that we raised a tall lateen sail. The question arose—What name or symbol we should paint on the sail. Because the paint penetrated the old canvas, we needed a name that read the same that was not only a palindrome but read the same directly and in the obverse. After a good deal of thought and discussion we hit upon *WOW*, which met all the requirements. But though the *WOW* gave us some good service, she was highly unstable and had a tendency to sail us right under. In spite of this the *WOW* gave us a new sense of the river and the elements that play upon it. The occasional foundering or capsize did not matter.

Tacking was a problem, because of the primitiveness of our gear. But we did learn how to make a point or two into the wind. Library books showed us how low we were on the evolutionary scale of the sailing boat.

Father was in two minds about the *WOW*. All too readily he saw its dangers, but he wanted us to get as much as possible out of Canada. Mother, more practical, bought a pair of cushions filled with Kapok to act as life savers. Jon was always the one for the conservation of our energies. One morning as we were paddling to Fitzroy Harbour (a distance of some thirty miles) we were overtaken by the *G.B. Greene*. She was towing an empty boom, having discharged the logs down the Deschenes Rapids. The opportunity for a tow was too much to be missed. By paddling hard we drew abreast of the end of the last log. We tied the canoe to it and settled down for a free ride in the summer sunshine. We were going quite fast, with the rocker arm of the *G.B. Greene*'s antique engine working furiously up and down, with a considerable bow wave. Then Jon decided he needed a pee. He prepared to climb out of the canoe into the boom. In so doing he tilted the canoe away from the boom. Thereupon our bow wave entered the canoe, overturning it and pitching me into the river. As I left the canoe I could see the axe and the frying pan going to the bottom, together with our two railway spikes, so useful in cooking over the camp fire. The sleeping bags, sustained by the air they contained, floated high.

The Central Canada Exhibition at Lansdowne Park came in August as the joys of idleness were beginning to wane and as the excitement of crowds and human variety was reasserting itself. A visit to the Exhibition involved streetcar journeys into town and out again. The day began with the excitement of anticipation, brought to a climax as you passed through the heavy iron turnstiles cold to the hand, to the sights, sounds and smells that only the Ex could produce, with the hours of discovery that lay ahead full of promise. The day ended with the queasy ride back to Britannia on a hot summer night with a stomach stuffed with popcorn, ice-cream, candy floss, hot dogs and Coca Cola, kept down by an effort of will. It was a point of pride not to throw up.

The things that drew us most were the entertainments on the Midway. They had a shabby glamour, being noisy and exotic, with milling crowds drawn by competitive brass-lunged barkers. There was a pumped-up exhilaration making of this assemblage of the tawdry and second rate a scene of shared excitement. The boxing booth challenged the local lads to do battle with the battered professionals. The pathetic freaks were depicted on the canvas fronts of their stalls. They did not interest us greatly, except the half-man half-woman, who, poor creature, was a great disappointment, partly because of the unconvincing nature of the phenomenon itself, but compounded by the restraint imposed by the Exhibition Committee. The hoochie-goochie girls with their seductive movements performed with a perfunctory weariness, seen by me as down-market versions of Salome dancing for John the Baptist's head. The try-your-strength machines, inviting candidates to ring the bell with a swing of the great wooden mallet, drew beefy men up to the limits of middle age, the younger ones to impress the girls and the older to prove themselves. There were silhouette cutters, one of whom with a few deft movements of his scissors made a passable likeness of our mother in her cloche hat; this profile Dad had framed. Less value for money were the sellers of potato peelers and other marvellous gadgets that never functioned in the home as they did when demonstrated amid flourishes and exhortations to buy. The demonstrators of such meretricious devices were expert in drawing a particular housewife in close to see how he was doing it, then engaging her directly in his patter, making it very difficult for her to withdraw without buying and so giving confidence to others.

Interspersed among the features of the Midway were the rides, blaring out their challenge to have yourself revolved, thrown about, hung upside down, bumped or dropped, but offering the possibility of intimate reassuring propinquity with your girl friend. On a smaller scale were the games of skill and chance, the shooting galleries, the coconut shies, the hooplah. Scattered about were the caravans of the show people, their open doors providing domestic glimpses of the nomads whose way of life this was.

But the mountebank offerings of the Midway, unknowingly reaching back to the fairs of the middle ages, were not the object of the Ex. Its main intent derived from the agricultural improvers of the Enlightenment of the eighteenth century when English squires and Scottish lairds had offered prizes for better husbandry. Under the aegis of the Ex the agriculture and home craft achievements of the Ottawa Valley were brought to the display areas under the grandstand and to the additional buildings provided by the Committees. Prize animals and agricultural machinery absorbed the knowing eyes of farmers, but most city folk passed them by without comprehension of the achievements and potential they embodied. So too with home made jams, preserves, bread and cakes and other products of the kitchen—they had their clientele among those for whom such things were important. There were handicrafts of all kinds, with sections for the young: my Spanish galleon won second prize in its section.

At the bandstand in the centre of the Park, and so free to all, there performed Creatore and his musicians. They were hired year after year from an agent in New York, with overtones of international celebrity. Creatore himself was, visually at least, and when seen at a distance, worth the money. He had long flowing hair, at that time taken to be a sure sign of musicianship. This was sometimes surmounted by a military cap in the manner of the great Sousa, but was sometimes allowed to flow free, especially when Creatore was conducting an aria from Verdi. There were plenty of histrionics in his Italianate conducting, his stout body and short arms going into rhythmic writhings and convulsions in his efforts to dispel the languor of some of his players. Closer up, however, Creatore lost his mystery—he seemed an exciteable little Italian, sweating profusely and without the air of command that came with distance.

The great highlight however of a day at the Ex was the grandstand show. A sign of growing up came when you switched from the matinee to the magic of the evening performances. In front of the large stage with its backcloth against the summer sky the band of the Governor General's Foot Guards in their scarlet tunics would provide the musical accompaniment. On would come the dancers, the acrobats, the singers. There would be an ascent by hot air balloon, a trapeze artist showing his skills as the contraption rose into the air. On one occasion, though we missed it, one of the men holding the rope to steady the balloon as it filled, being the worse for drink, did not let go when the others did and so was carried aloft, dropping to two broken legs. There was also a kind of polo played by men in Ford chassis with rollbars, using a vast ball some five feet high: this, with its possibility of collisions, locked wheels and roll-overs was much more exciting than the trotting races that interspersed the acts. The climax might be a high dive into a small tank of water with a blazing surface. Fireworks would mark the end of the evening, and, in a sense, the end of the summer.

CHAPTER 7

Over McGregor's Grocery Store

In 1924, we moved to 227 Bank Street at the corner of Lisgar. It was a modest place for a home but it served us during the winter. Summers were spent a tram ride away in Britannia, at the cottage.

Our apartment was immediately above McGregor's grocery store, then one of the quality purveyors to the capital. It still proudly displayed on its window the Vice-Regal arms 'By Appointment to the Governor General' and retained a reputation for its sausages under the slogan 'Six to the Pound'. Any boy in Ottawa called McGregor could expect to be called 'Sausages'. Indeed there was a painting of the sausages on our exterior wall on the Lisgar side. Close by was a counter-weighted fire escape, the steps of which would lower gently to the sidewalk if anyone had the confidence to commit themselves to them. Around the two street sides of Apartment 9, just below our windows, there ran a cornice on the face of which was a continuous sign proudly bearing McGregor's name and extolling the merits of his store. Mother used this ledge as a refrigerator in winter, placing on it whatever needed to be kept cool.

This was to be our home for nine years, until I was seventeen and ready to leave high school. It is the place of deepest memories, the scene that returns in dreams unbidden. It is where boyhood possessions are located in memory—the Meccano set, the toy steam engine, the clockwork train, the magic lantern, lead soldiers, Punch and Judy puppets, boxing gloves and cars, trucks and fire engines made in Hong Kong from enamelled tin. Nearly all the furniture was second hand, much of it pretty battered. But there were three glass fronted bookcases in which father proudly displayed his books. It is the place where we passed from the androgyny of innocence and acceptance (on the surface at least) to the questionings and assertions of adolescence.

The ostensible reason for our move was to gain more room. But there was not much more of that. The kitchen, with its oilcloth-covered table by the window which looked out onto Lisgar and Bank was the heart of the family, where meals were taken (except on Sundays), discussions and arguments with father held (often post-prandial), and homework done. From the kitchen window you could see the clock face in the coal merchant's window opposite: thus F.W. Bargue and Co. provided our time-piece. The biggest room was the parlour, where stood the Damascus table and other relics. In the middle of the room was a sizeable square table, somewhat unstable, on which we had Sunday dinner after morning church. There was a green tasselled sofa under one window while nearby our first telephone stood on top of the bookshelves that held the novels. There were two bedrooms, separated by a wall of a single course of bricks, one for our parents and Kenny, and one for Eddie and I. Under our parents' bed was Dad's filing system, consisting of a number of orange boxes. These contained old manilla envelopes, each labelled with the name of some newsworthy person and containing relevant clippings. Dad always complained that *The Citizen* had no 'morgue' or reference system, so that he had to provide his own.

There was a bathroom with no external window, and a cupboard of some size under the stairs. This latter had a dual function. The back part was stuffed with string-tied bundles of *The British Weekly*, the nonconformist newspaper which had helped to form father's character and outlook on the world from his early manhood, which was now sent with unfailing regularity from Birmingham by his sister, the devoted Louise. She also enclosed *The Sunday Companion*, a genteel publication for ladies. The stories of these journals seemed to us to be concerned entirely with personable young ministers, who, with no sign of physical passion, but after mild travails consisting of mis-understandings, transparent to the most simple-minded of readers, or parental obtuseness of a monumental kind, won the nicest girl in the congregation. Whereas *The Sunday Companion* was expendable, *The British Weekly* was not, hence its growing bulk at the back of the cupboard. At the front was my workbench, consisting of the crate from Damascus, on which I was to produce my masterpiece, a Spanish galleon, from a design in the *Boy's Own Paper*.

The hallway was a feature of the apartment, wide enough to hold a two-doored wardrobe at one end and long enough to get a kick at a football. Dad would play goalie, for the wardrobe doors made a terrible noise if struck by a missed shot. Mother had by the time I was ten taken to going early to bed to read. She would tolerate the football game for an hour or so, the ball often ricocheting off her door adjacent to the goal. But finally would come a quiet voice 'That's enough, please', and the noise would cease, with Dad looking a little sheepish.

We enjoyed the fact that we could make a good deal of noise of an evening, because there was only the empty store beneath us. But as we got older we became a little ashamed of our home. The thing that contributed most to this was getting rid of the garbage. There was no proper system so that cabbage leaves, potato peelings and tea leaves had to be rolled in newspaper and this ghastly cylinder carried along the hall and down the stairs into Bank Street, along the front of the store and then into Lisgar, to be finally deposited in the alleyway along with the garbage of the store. For doing this we each received 25 cents per week, going into Mr. McGregor's glass-paned office to claim it. But the job was not worth the money, for we were haunted by the fear of meeting someone we knew, or of the parcel succumbing to its wetness and dropping part of its contents on the sidewalk.

In one sense we definitely came up in the world: we proudly acquired a telephone. It was one of those upright affairs, a foot high column of black bakelite with an earpiece, 'the receiver', which you held in your left hand. When it was lifted a pleasant female voice inquired 'Number please?', to which you had only to recite the number, knowing, as shown on the movies, that she was sitting at her console amid a bank of fellow operators making the necessary connection. In those happy pre-dial days it was not long before we learned how the telephone could be used as a lethal weapon. It happened that Dad's friend having built a wall with the assistance of our gang, decided to reward the four of us with a visit to the movies. The Regent was showing an early horror film for which we enthusiastically opted. It was called 'Whispering Wires'. A madman seeking revenge on a gallery of his enemies had lured them to an isolated country house where he practiced advanced technology on them. He would insert an explosive charge in the telephone earpiece, call his victim from a phone rigged in the bushes in the grounds, and then (after appropriate gloatings), place the earpiece to the mouthpiece, thus causing the lethal charge to detonate. The film was thoroughly moral, for the telephone murderer was able to kill only palpably evil men before our hero, in defence of our heroine, stopped him. But the film must have been a nightmare for the telephone exchange with hordes of kids like ourselves hurrying home to see what happened when mouthpiece spoke to earpiece. The answer, of course was a screaming feedback.

As at the Wilkies, we had little to do with the neighbours; indeed we hardly knew who they were. To this there were two exceptions. At the head of the stairs was the Prince Costume Company, run by a young widow. When the door of her apartment was ajar we could see racks containing fancy dress of all kinds, with the occasional glimpse of a lady being done up as Carmen or a gent trying on a Mephistopheles suit. At Hallow e'en the stairs seemed full of people bearing away their fantasy identities.

More important in our lives was our neighbour whose door faced us across the hall. This was Mrs. Blower, now well up in her seventies.

She had run a boarding house for many years, which had once indeed harboured the young Mackenzie King before he became a politician and Canada's prime minister. In her widow's weeds and jade necklace she was strongly reminiscent of Queen Victoria and had indeed something of a regal bearing. Though not unkindly; she had a basilisk stare that could be frightening. This however was counteracted by the wattles of her neck which she had the habit of flapping to and fro with her right hand, making it hard for Eddie and me, once we had compared notes on the subject, to keep our faces straight. Being a strong, almost ferocious supporter of the Church of England, she was visited regularly by Archdeacon Iremonger who amazed us. He carried up the stairs of 227 Bank Street the aura of Trollope's Barchester, complete with gaiters and shovel hat.

Mother would pay occasional calls on Mrs. Blower, sometimes taking us with her. Eddie and I would sit on her solemn straight-backed pseudo-Jacobean chairs, the pride of her former boarding house, listening to the conversation, sprinkled sometimes with recollections of the Prime Minister as a young man. There were two delicate subjects that were carefully but regularly skirted around. Mother would say, 'I do hope, Mrs. Blower, that our boys do not make too much noise for you?' Mrs. B. accepting the propitiation, would reassure mother that we were no trouble. We would marvel at this, for on Sunday nights when our parents had gone to church we would sometimes raise an unholy row, playing football in the hall, have the phonograph full on or mount a fight with rolled up newspapers. Our front door bell had long since disappeared, leaving a circular aperture: through this we would take turns to peer at Mrs. Blower's door opposite. She for her part would open it, glare in indignation at ours, hesitate and then withdraw.

The other touchy subject was cockroaches. The apartment was full of them, teaming at nights, especially in our kitchen, adjacent to that of Mrs. Blower. It was one of our pleasures to hold cockroach raids, suddenly switching on the kitchen lights and slapping about with rolled-up newspapers. A variant was to capture a prime example and then test on it the effectiveness of 'Sappho', an insecticide of the day. We would puff out of the container a cone of the stuff an inch or two high on top of our victim; there would be signs of movement and it would emerge in full vigour, making for cover. Both mother and Mrs. Blower believed the other to be responsible for the cockroach population. Mother's case was that the old lady, who roasted chickens for sale in McGregor's below, had generated conditions highly favourable to cockroaches; Mrs. Blower in her turn thought they were our fault. This gave rise to conversational exchanges of which Eddie and

I became connoisseurs, both ladies lamenting the presence of the creatures, but keeping their respective theories as oblique as possible.

The apartment met the needs of Dad's job—as a journalist he was well-placed in the centre of Ottawa, able to move easily about his beat. In spite of the irregular hours and the nervous tension, he enjoyed his work, revelling in being in the know, talking to men of authority in the little civic world of Ottawa and in the larger world of Parliament Hill, savouring his own small element of power as a dispenser of publicity. He liked being a member of a group of men who, though also often in the position of suppliants for news, were also freebooters— pickers up of other people's property in the form of information, and not above using it to swap for alternative information so that a story had been made and an enmity avoided. But he was in a kind of permanent dilemma in coming to terms with such tactics. In a small city based upon jealousy in politics and a status-conscious civil service, together with a diplomatic community on the alert for slights to dignity, it was inevitable, as the years passed that he should become increasingly cynical of publicity seeking, attempts to suppress indiscretions and touchiness over precedence. Though the profession of evangelist had yielded to that of reporter, much of the former man remained. He was a campaigning teetotaler, an enemy of gambling, a member of the Committee of the Bible Society and a deacon of his church, all of which activities were at a discount in the newsroom. He was tried briefly on *The Citizen* softball team against *The Journal*. At left field, with the bases loaded, he made a splendid catch, but then disaster, as he in the manner of an English cricketer, tossed the ball high in the air in triumph while *The Journal* team cleared its bases.

Like other reporters he had a deep distrust of university graduates in newspaper work, seeing them as privileged youths trying to take a short-cut into a profession that had to be learned on the job. Only 'on the street' was it possible to acquire 'a nose for news'. He continued his own self-education by wide reading, especially in the field of biography. He delighted most in short biographical essays by the English journalists A.G. Gardiner and E.T. Raymond; indeed the 'profile' was the form of human expression he most admired. He could conduct an interview with the world's great as they briefly materialised in Ottawa. If they came from the Old Country with which he identified, he could often approach them in terms of his own experience. Nothing pleased him more than to be told by his editor: 'Hey, Syd, get down to the Chateau and interview so-and-so.'

He had always the hope that, in his outpost, he might extract from one of the great some gem of insight or indiscretion that would reverberate through the world's press, and even find its way into

15   S T Checkland, the author's father, at home *c.*1933.

biography or anthology. But his reading and reflection got in the way. He often knew so much about the subject in hand that when doing a book review or a 'Saturday Special' for *The Citizen* he congested it, clotting his writing with parentheses and gratuitous references. There was, too, a certain lack of self-confidence: he would quote from his books or his files when another would have appropriated such material disguised in paraphrase. But he could sometimes score with a telling expression: in a piece on the annual Exhibition (or Fair), dealing with the belly dancers billed as the 'Baghdad Beauties', he described them as being as far from the one as from the other.

But he knew what made 'good copy', and had an instinct for the local human interest story. He believed in an absolute distinction between 'the news' and the expression of opinion. In the news columns there should be an objective account of what happened, with no interpretation to intrude. The latter was to be confined strictly to the editorial page. The rule in reporting the news was that in the first sentence there should be, as he put it, a statement of 'what, where, why and how'. This, of course, was all very well in reporting a crime or a fire, but was less effective where human responses, ambitions and enmities were involved. Ottawa as a civil service town was full of tender susceptibilities, containing a kind of super petty bourgeoisie, based not upon shopkeeping and the like, but on position, status and the hope of promotion.

Father distrusted grand phrases when used of the press, like 'the Fourth Estate', but he believed it had great power and responsibility. He knew, too, how difficult it was to maintain integrity. His own efforts to do so were one reason why he never became more than a reporter on the beat. More than once he refused to introduce more 'colour' into a story than he believed justified. One such occasion had to do with the appearance in Ottawa of an evangelical faith healer. Dad had a deep distrust of such activity, possibly fearing the element of hysteria it involved. He recounted the dramatic scenes in a flat prose that drained away any claim to the miraculous, flatly refusing his editor's plea that he brighten up his account.

Like others who have undertaken an archival role, father found it difficult to keep the files of his 'morgue' up to date. The clippings piled up remorselessly. He tried to interest his sons in this project tempting us with the inducement of a small increase in pocket money. We were not impressed. School provided enough of the disciplined, non-optional activity. Dad's filing system continued to pile up unchecked under the bed.

On the way home from Elgin Street School we usually passed along Metcalfe Street. When I was nine years old I had there my first encounter with death, apart from the corpses fished out of the water onto Britannia pier. Like many other children of immigrants, having no family other than our parents, we made no acquaintance with old age or death; fate in Metcalfe Street provided the occasion. There was a long queue of people outside one of the large houses, number 252, slowly filing into it. Out of curiosity I made my way with the rest up the steps and through the door, to find myself passing the bier of an ancient man. Though I did not know it, this was the corpse of James Rudolphus Both, the lumber king. There he lay, aged 98, in his open coffin of solid bronze, his head slightly raised on a small velvet cushion. His flowing beard seemed to reach almost to his waist; its silken whiteness clashed with the brown blotches and purple veins in his tiny folded hands. Over all there hung a smell of over-sweet flowers mingling with the final decay of the shrunken mannikin. The scene brought recurrent nightmares, in which terrible Old Testament prophets from engravings transmuted into J.R. Both and vice-versa, passing in and out of the high arched gate of death, threatening and decomposing.

Father told us who he was. This was the man who had worked 4,250 square miles of timber limits between the Ottawa River and Georgian Bay, enough land to make a strip a mile wide reaching across

Canada from the Atlantic to the Pacific. He had run what had been one of the world's largest one-man businesses; he had married one of his daughters to a European prince. He was the Croesus of the Ottawa Valley. There was profound respect for a man who from humble beginnings and through many setbacks, could extract a fortune from the wilderness, who had acted on the grand baronial scale, who stood for the high days of pioneering. The newspaper headlines extolled a life of 'Industry, Foresight and Thrift'. The public was told that 'No one man had contributed more than he to the march of progress in Canada'.

That he had helped to imprison the Chaudière Falls, whose might the Indians had propitiated with tribute, and which Champlain had so admired; that he had operated ruthlessly on the environment; that the granting to one man of such an empire was an inappropriate outcome of the political process; that his rewards were far greater than his contribution, and that he had left his sons in a dynastic position; all these matters were not mentioned. In the Canada of the 1920s, long-run concern for resources had hardly begun. To be able, as Both had done, to extract generous concessions from politicians, was regarded in an ambivalent light: in principle it was wrong, but there was admiration for the man who could do it, mounting more than proportionately with his success. Inequalities of wealth arising from the exploitation of natural resources were made acceptable by an intuitive feeling that, at the stage of things reached in Canada in Both's time, men of great energy and persistence should be allowed to reap the economies of scale, even though it be at the expense of a non-renewable asset and a major attack upon nature. It had been long forgotten that our forebears in the great forests of northern Europe had cherished their wooded inheritance for centuries, honouring the spirit that dwelt in each tree: before felling one they would ask its permission and would placate its spirit by attaching its crown to the top of any structure built with it.

Though J.R. Both was my first direct acquaintance with death, there was another sense in which it crept into our consciousness. This had to do with war. Though the war to end wars had been fought, war was a kind of background accompaniment to our childhood lives. When very young we had joined with other kids in chanting in honour of victory

> 'Ar soldiers went to war
> 'Ar soldiers won
> 'Ar soldiers stuck their bayonets
> Up the Kaiser's ...
> 'Ar Soldiers

This bellicosity survived, as for example, when a war film was shown at a children's matinee the movie house would resound to cheers as a wave of attacking Germans was mown down by machine-gun fire. But the thought of what such things really meant slowly dawned, especially when the films, such as *All Quiet on the Western Front*, began to show us the tragedy of men on both sides caught up in forces which they could not resist. The annual Remembrance Day service in First Baptist Church brought home the feelings of the bereaved as the minister stood under the brass plate on the church wall and read out with great deliberation the full names of the fallen to the subdued sobbing of the women. The notes of the Last Post became almost unbearably poignant as they were picked out on the keyboard of the church organ, not so much as a hero's farewell as on the battlefield, but as a lament for lost love and promise destroyed. We saw the veterans each year at the armistice parade, men in what father called mufti (their best suits and overcoats), a few moving stiffly and some with an empty sleeve marching in step with the rest, those further back shuffling their feet in an effort to find a lost rhythm. All wore medals that clinked and flashed on their dark coats. Most, like father (though he never marched) had been awarded two, the service medal and the victory medal, though a few men who had been professional soldiers or who had served in the Boer War had a braver display. Brigadier General John T. Winkler, his white moustache flowing in the best imperial manner, a kind of Holywood version of a British general, was near the head of the parade. To us entering our teens these men, mostly perhaps in their late thirties or early forties, seemed old and set. Their long lines soon bored us, for we wanted to see the 'real' soldiers, those who had been boys while the fighting was going on, especially the Cameron Highlanders led by their pipers. We could too easily forget that through these men Canada had played her part at the testing of nations on the most terrible of human battlefields.

Mixed in with all this was a kind of war nostalgia. At the far end of the long narrow cupboard at the cottage which separated our bedroom from that of our parents were bits of Dad's war gear. There were gunny sacks and packs, a helmet, a cap, bits of webbing equipment and an old army manual. Much of this stuff bore Dad's army number which, by some quirk is still engraved on the memory (246019). The manual had stiff brown covers, slightly convex from lying somewhere in the sun. It told you how to do all manner of things in order that large bodies of men could live under minimal conditions—how to make latrines, how to improvise field kitchens, how to erect bivouacs. In short the manual embodied the field wisdom of British armies all over the world, probably going back to the Duke of Wellington's time. It was illustrated with fine line drawings. There was no gas mask, though father would tell us how lethal the stuff was, recounting how that when in training in the gas chamber a comrade had fumbled in changing from his standard mask to his emergency one. He had taken a compulsive panicky breath and had slumped to the floor, only to be saved by quick hospital treatment. We never really knew why these relics of Dad's war service had survived: perhaps he had wanted us to sense that part of his experience just as with the Holyland bag. He took us to see R.C. Sherriff's play 'Journey's End', set in a dugout; it was some days thereafter before he could discuss it with us. He would sing the old war songs to us, like 'Pack up your troubles in your old kit bag' and 'It's a long way to Tipperary', but he would not sing

> *O death where is thy sting-a-ling-a-ling?*
> *O grave thy victory?*

Our attitudes to war were confused by those of our elders. At school we wrote juvenile essays for competitions organised by the League of Nations Society in which we dilated on the futility of men seeking to destroy one another and bringing to bear the fearful capacity of advanced industrialisation to do so. But in the Elgin Street School playground we were drilled as cadets presumably to prepare us for the next time round. In church we rejoiced that the Old Testament God of Battles had blessed the arms of the Israelites, in spite of what the Remembrance Service taught us of the costs of victory. In any case, who did our elders think we were going to fight? The United States as an enemy was inconceivable. This left only Europe and future disturbers of the peace there. Or was any specified putative enemy required at all? Were we doing our childish drill in the playground as a response to some deeply engrained but generalised sense that all nations should be ready to fight should the need arise, and that males should never lose the warrior instinct?

The School Board maintained Mr. Collins, often referred to honourifically as 'Captain Collins', to move from school to school, to drill us in the playground. He wore an officer's tunic, but without badges of rank. He was a real exponent of the parade ground manner, demonstrating postures and movements with marvellous stampings and wheelings, shouting the orders to himself. To keep time for us when marching he carried the school handbell at his side, between his hip and his rigidly extended left arm, using his hand to move the clapper of the bell, producing a marvellously regular clicking sound. Because it was not very loud he would march alongside us, shouting orders. Our military training at Elgin got no further than forming up and marching about, but presumably our elders thought this a useful first step. Inevitably there was a day of demonstration. By this time we had been 'officered' by the boys who had distinguished themselves, moving and marching to voices that were on the point of breaking or which had only lately passed it.

By the time of the annual school parade it was spring and we were commuting by streetcar to Britannia. Dad had organised us into a soccer team of five to play against boys who lived around the Grove, near the Old and New Mills. Dad was referee, shrilling his whistle and running up and down, delivering verdicts on the rules and stopping the play in order to give instructions on how to improve your game. My brother was fiercely competitive, involving much elbow and body work and the occasional tripping. Dad would descend on him, ordering penalty kicks and threatening to send him off; indeed, there were homeric battles with a purple-faced Dad upholding English canons of fairplay and the dignity of refereeship against a son whose only priority was to win.

We began to become interested in what went on at the Lakeside Gardens, Britannia's dance hall. It was a vast white wooden building shaped like an aircraft hanger with its high curved tarpaper roof, 200 feet long and 75 feet wide, visible at a great distance from out in the lake. Along both sides there were shutters that were opened on summer evenings. From these floated the sounds of the dance bands. To get a view of the interior you climbed a telegraph pole conveniently placed to give a good view of the band and the dance floor. Clustered on the pole we could see the lanterns, the coloured lighting, the perspiring but rhythmic musicians and the couples clinging to one another as they moved. We had heard father tell of a cousin who had made a disastrous marriage, having met 'her' in a dance hall: could this be the kind of place where the sins of the flesh, obliquely dilated upon in church, had their origins? Father condemned it as a firetrap.

Ottawa in August 1926 declared itself to be one hundred years old. Approaching the age of ten, like other children, I did not ponder on the nature of public celebrations as part of the search for a communal persona. But Ottawa in seeking to define its historical identity had something of a problem. The hundred years was rather like what Huck Finn would have called a 'stretcher', for the place, having received its first settlers led by Philemon Wright in 1826 had been simply a lumber depot and the head of the Rideau Canal System for its first forty years until made the capital of Canada in 1867. The river had, of course, been important as the explorers' and *voyageurs*' route to the interior, but there was little to be said about what had happened along its banks, for little folk lore was available. The woods were not storied places as in Germany, but had indeed been cut ruthlessly away. The Algonquin Indians had produced no culture to rival that of their exploiters the Iroquois, and had been largely exterminated or expelled from the Valley. As a capital the city became the point of convergence of Canada's regional politicians. But the Canadian drama had largely been enacted elsewhere with the Reiel Rebellion in Manitoba, the building of the railways across the Continent and the service of the Royal Canadian Mounted Police in the North West Territories. The true Canadian exemplification of modern urban experience lay in Montreal and Toronto. Certainly Ottawa had been the scene of Sir John A. Macdonald's dominion forging and Sir Wilfrid Laurier's attempt at American reciprocity, but the old Scotch ruffian and the urbane French Canadian were difficult to project as drama, especially when drama requires the development of the seamier and conflicting side of things, a mode inconsistent with celebratory blandness. Nevertheless the city put on a brave show. There was an historical pageant, celebrating the 'Spirit of the Chaudière', the explorations of Champlain, the pioneers of the Ottawa Valley, together with highlights of the greater moments on the Hill. A military tattoo and fireworks demonstrated the precision and verve of the City's largely amateur soldiery. The whole was blessed by a visit from the Right Reverend A.F. Winnington-Ingram, Bishop of London. Dad reported his sermon in crowded Christ Church Cathedral sitting on the pulpit steps.

But the occasion we enjoyed most was the Old Time Parade, three miles long, passing below our windows. We had guests, sitting with us at our windows to watch the spectacle. At the appointed time we were in position. Across the street was a low building the flat top of which was more or less on a level with our windows. On it sat the family and friends of the operator of the doughnut business below. (This featured in its window a machine that never lost its fascination for us: it was glass-sided, revealing a mechanism which squirted rings of dough into hot fat so that they swelled and browned to doughnuts before your very eyes). Both we and the doughnut party, the parade being delayed, began to get restless. Our friend suggested to father that they should put on an entertainment for our eye-level neighbours across the street. Dad responded by producing the Holyland bag. He donned the scarlet fez while Mr. B. put on the yashmak, wrapping a towel over his head. Draped in sheets they then faced each other at the window, going through the semblance of a marital quarrel, using the window as a procenium arch. The party across the street became aware of the spectacle, nudged one another and watched with wrapt attention, commenting in great seriousness. We boys marvelled that Dad could play up so well to Mr. B's lead, gesticulating, wringing his hands and threatening with his fists, while Mr. B. bobbed about, shook his head, shrugged and wagged an admonitory finger.

The following August Ottawa resounded to a much grander occasion, the Diamond Jubilee of Confederation. It was sixty years ago, in 1867, as we were repeatedly told at school, that the Fathers of Confederation had gathered together from all the British North American Colonies and had founded our great Dominion extending from sea to sea. Their group portrait, showing them in various statesmen-like postures, from the heroic to the pensive, with their leader Sir John A. Macdonald standing in their midst, featured in our schoolroom, and became engraved in memory. It was our equivalent of the American school child's portrayal of the signatories of the Declaration of Independence, sharing the idiom of human (all male) sagacity and disinterestedness. The dominant themes of the celebrations were the forging of unity out of diversity, the sinking of differences in the interests of a greater good and the creation of a nation on a continental scale. Our elders, especially perhaps the politicians, needed to reassure themselves that a national identity did really exist, embracing the recalcitrant French who still remembered the conscription issue, and the European incomers with their own diverse cultures who had so recently helped to populate the prairies. We each received a copper medal at school in honour of the occasion.

The frustration of Sir John and his colleagues of American expansionism northward was hinted at, though the undefended 3,000 mile frontier shared between the nations was commended to us and to the world as a model of peaceful coexistence. Our prevailing air of prosperity owed much to the buoyant performance of the American economy. The visit of the hero of the Atlantic, Colonel Lindberg, flying into Ottawa in his plane *The Spirit of St. Louis*, stood for American vigour and daring. But the tone of the celebrations was strongly British. We dimly thought that 'Land of Hope and Glory', so frequently played, had been composed with Canada in mind. We sang with great earnestness about

> *The Mapull leaf,*
> *Our Emblum dear*

with its reference to Wolfe, that 'dauntless hero', who

> *Planted firm Britannia's flag*
> *On Canada's fair domain*

adding, without sensitivity to French Canadian feelings, and in bland, dismissal of what Quebec nationalists called 'soixante ans d'injustice',

Here may it rest
Our boast, our pride

Patriotic songs are curiously child-like compositions, the work of elders, revealing earnest aspirations and a desire for reassurance about identity too embarrassing to be stated in any other form, approved of if not commissioned by officialdom and learned by heart by inquiring infants. 'Canada, My Home' proclaimed the world's intense concern with Canada's performance:

Still onward, upward to fame
All nations thee shall proclaim
A land of wealth and liberty
Whose homes are filled with joy
Rule, rule with power and with might
Thou whose hopes are so bright ...

The Ottawa schools were assembled on the great day on the lawns of Parliament Hill. With our contingent submerged in the mass of childhood we sang the patriotic songs we had been taught, fidgeted through the speeches, joined in prayers of thankfulness and national humility, and heard the carillon, brought from the bellfounders in Belgium and installed in the resplendent new Peace Tower, ring out over the city.

The press had tried to name it the Victory Tower, a last echo of the triumphalism of the post-war years, but it became the Peace Tower, containing the nation's sorrowing memorial to its war dead. The new building now being dedicated was a modified Phoenix, with lines that were cleaner both vertically and horizontally than its Victorian predecessor. Fire had permitted the Canadian parliament to escape from British railway Gothic into something distinctive and worthy of the future. But Gothicism, so largely purged from the exterior, was vigorously reasserted inside the great arch on which the tower rested. There the stonemasons were given their heraldic head. The parliamentary library, so like a spiky wedding cake, had survived the fire and so stood as a link with the Fathers of Confederation. It nestled intact behind the Peace Tower on the bluff above the Ottawa River where Colonel By had built his barracks, an octagonal fantasy with its aerial buttresses, a nightmare for librarians (being incapable of extension), but a marvellous complement to the linearity of the main building and the tower. A shaft of stone-clad steel surged upward to a new height, worthy of the consciousness of a people who had so lately helped to shape the fate of other nations far away. The composition seen from the lawns now bore a new dash of the chateau style while around its back the library suggested the middle ages, echoing the Catholic cathedrals of the forest lands of northern Europe. 'The Westminster of the Wilderness', as Ottawa had been called at the time of Confederation, now had a worthy focus. Its architects, past and present, had done better for the nation than its song writers. But it was the singing of the songs that was our business, not the contemplation of the architecture, though the tower did indeed seem a marvel, especially when it spoke with its bells.

There was also a spectacle in the Auditorium. The usual ice hockey, of the Ottawa Senators, and the wrestling, gave place for one night to a pageant. To this we of Elgin Street School provided a mass minuet. Whether this was intended to celebrate the grace of eighteenth century England or the doomed aristocrats of pre-revolutionary France was not made clear. The girls were done up as ladies of fashion and allowed a measure of precocious cosmetics. My costume, made by mother, was excellent, but the cotton wool wig, as Eddie remarked, looked like a tea cosy. Admiring parents would not, however, allow such an occasion to topple over into bathos, though it was a marvel to see some of the tougher boys going through the ballroom movements of the age of elegance, as to the manner born.

16   Mother spent her evenings reading in bed, c.1937.

Young children think of their parents as equal to any effort, and indestructable. The early teens may bring the first doubts. This was so with us. Mother disappeared into hospital. We were not told why. Dad took us for our meals to Bowles Lunch in Sparks Street, next to the *Citizen*, one of the nerve centres of his own information network. We enjoyed ourselves in this one-arm joint where you placed your food on the widened right arm of your chair, close to the counter so that you could hear the Damon Runyon character taking orders and shouting them back to the kitchen, translating a glass of milk into 'let it rain', and poached eggs on toast as 'two on a raft'. But there was an underlying unease that mother should be withdrawn from us. We went with Dad to fetch her from the hospital. We overheard her thanking the nurse, and, a little later, saying to father how pleasant the nurse had been, ending, half jokingly with the words, 'She would make for you a good second wife'. For though the doctor, having performed a mastectomy, had said that the signs were good, the shadow of cancer had come, our first intimation of mortality.

CHAPTER 8

Odyssey to the Old Country

With mother's condition apparently stabilised, life settled down once more. But not for long. Early in 1928 father decided that Ed and I were old enough to benefit from a visit to the Old Country. There was not enough money for all five of us to go; moreover such a party would be too large to impose on the relatives who would provide most of the accommodation. It was agreed that mother and Kenny should stay at home, to go to England in a few years time, and that father would lead Eddie and I in a voyage of discovery. This would bring father up to date for journalistic purposes, as well as being highly educative for us.

So in the spring the preparations began. Planning was done of course by father. In retrospect it is clear that in this, his fiftieth year, he proposed to demonstrate to us the wonder of the places in England and Scotland that had so engrained themselves in him. That there was a real measure of self-indulgence on his part there can be no doubt. There was also a desire at a certain level of consciousness to show us where our roots lay, and to provide correctives and enrichments to the Canadian way of life. So it was that in July, when I was eleven rising twelve, we embarked on what was to be eight weeks of travel. It was a pre-adolescent odyssey in which the mind, unconsciously at the time, was to store in its depths images of England and Scotland that are still instantly recoverable.

Our mounting excitement before departure was carefully hidden from our parents. It centred upon the coloured deck plans, the luggage labels and the new clothes so carefully bought by mother at the spring sales. At last the expectation gave way to the sight of the SS *Montcalm* towering over her berth at Montreal. We became proprietorial at once, rushing about the ship. There were mysterious ship smells, with their admixtures of tar and paint; the deck planking gleamed in the sun, the polished brass, the teak handrails, the great funnels, the splendour of the lounges and dining rooms, the treacherously raised thresholds, the harsh steel of the bulkhead doors with their heavy levers to secure them shut. The white lifeboats echoed this hint of danger, but the portholes with their massive threaded clamps, secure against any sea,

17   Edward and Sydney on board the SS *Montcalm*, Summer 1928.

provided reassurance. Following the deck signs we soon found our
cabin, tried the taps on the tiny washbasin and climbed onto the bunks.

Passing down the St. Lawrence we stared fascinated at the villages
along the shore, with their silver-spired churches and their clustered
dwellings, resplendent in the sun, separated by the long narrow farmsteads running back from the shore into the hinterland, just as our
schoolbooks had said. This was the real land of the *habitant*, Canada's
inheritance from pre-revolutionary peasant Europe. There came to
mind one of our history lessons in which the teacher had contrasted
the dour Scotsmen of the Hudson's Bay Company, steadfast and alone
in the northern wilderness, with the Frenchman strung along the St.
Lawrence, 'who likes to feel his neighbour's elbow'.

The citadel at Quebec, one of the world's great stone fortresses, came into view with its aura of Wolfe and Montcalm, two captains *sans peur et sans reproche*, united in death in battle, thus sharing in the chivalric legend of our schooling—an effort made by the victors at reconciliation between the races. At the foot of the bluff stood old Quebec, where Jacques Cartier and Samuel de Champlain, servants of the King of France, had wintered in the wilderness, uneasy about the Indians and wondering where the great waterway led. It was in passing to and from England along the St. Lawrence that we got this our only view of the heartland of French Canada, seeing it in the picturesqueness of distance and through the glass of what we had been taught. Shortly after passing Belle Isle icebergs appeared, those elemental fragments of Canada's icepack, moving slowly southward, silent and fantastical, neither land nor sea, passively menacing, casting a chill on the air as ghosts are reputed to do, but somehow beautiful as their basic whiteness reflected the blues and greens of sky and water.

By this time the old hands among the passengers, with the aid of a senior steward, were canvassing names for the ship's concert. Father, following his journalist instinct, got a copy of the passenger list fresh from the ship's printer. There were a few British MPs and indeed two lords, with names redolent of Eton and Harrow and Oxford and Cambridge. We had soon discovered the stiff class basis of transatlantic

18   Iceberg at Belle Isle along the St. Lawrence, Summer 1928.

travel, with those of the first class occupying the foredeck clear of the fumes of the funnels, having their own superior lounge and dining room, with cabins at promenade deck level, an ambience of good tailoring and *hauts couture*, where formal dress for dinner was *de rigeur*. Here there was space and grace, together with stewards of an extraordinary degree of deference. Here was social stratification in its most obvious form. We were part of a shipful of folk with two modes of life, sharply distinguished. We learned that if you entered upon this social territory with confidence, ignoring the signs which said 'First Class Passengers Only', you could share it.

Looking out from beside the helmsman one could view the Atlantic as he saw it, inspect the compasses and charts that made sense of the featureless expanse. There was too the signalling system, with its levers that told the engineers, blind in the bowels of the ship, what to do with their immense engines. On the bridge all was order and alertness, presided over by confidence clothed in immaculate uniforms. Steel gangways, grilled walkways and steep ladder-like steps brought us to a world of loud and relentless thumping and humming below the waterline artificially lit and ventilated, a place of sweating men in overalls moving about with oily rags in their hands, presiding over their vast power units. The propellor shafts ran half the length of the ship, revolving with great power and speed, yet so true and shiny as to seem almost motionless as they thrust us forward.

The ship's concert was the grand social event in which we celebrated that brief sense of identity that unites the passengers on a sea voyage. Mr. Stirk, a rotund manager in the Co-op of Birmingham, presided. Just as he was about to begin his speech of welcome, a party of first-class passengers rustled in wearing evening dress, making possible a mutual inspection of the otherwise segregated. There were the standard baritone and soprano solos (including 'On the road to Mandalay', 'Roses of Picardy', and 'Drink to me only with thine eyes'), with generous encores; there was Irish clog dancing (indeed two bouts of it, one by girls and one by pneumatically nimble matrons accompanied by a single wiry grannie); there was amateur conjuring; there were recitations, including 'Excelsior'. The occasion was one for the unself-conscious performer; the ship's concert was indeed a relic of the age of the Irish and Highland *ceilidh*. To stiffen the proceedings there was a steward from Liverpool of perhaps semi-professional quality, who acted as a stand-up comedian. His climactic turn was at the piano, demonstrating the ludicrous side of grand opera. He played an expiring heroine melodiously calling for help, together with her hero, she trilling, 'I am drowning! I am drowning!', and he booming the reiterated and unhurried response 'I will save thee! I will save thee!'

On the seventh day we stood off the west coast of Ireland at Clew Bay, County Mayo, overlooked by the revered mountain, Croagh Patrick, the Sinai of Ireland where the Saint had engaged in prayer and fasting for forty days and forty nights some 1500 years before. The solitary grandeur of its cone was invisible to us, for night, and a light mist enclosed it. A large group of our passengers were pilgrims to this holy place, intending to join the climb up the mountain on the last Sunday in July, performing the penitential 'stations'. The plan was that the ship should enter the Bay and that the pilgrims should be taken off by tender. Some were Irish-Americans. Among them was a priest who had been so bitter about the British record in Ireland that Eddie and I feared that father might confront him: this crisis was avoided because the priest's anti-British sentiments were uttered mostly in the bar, a place that was shunned by Dad. The liner nosed her way into the island-strewn bay, with a considerable sea running. The tender appeared from the darkness, came alongside and moved up and down the ship's side like a demented elevator. The reception party from Westport in their best suits negotiated the rocking gangplank, carefully timing their moves. There were lengthy speeches of welcome in the lounge, after which the pilgrims had no choice but to show their faith in the Saint by passing to the tender. They were justified, for in the course of the speeches in which St. Patrick had been so much invoked, the sea had calmed somewhat. As the ship crept back to sea the mountain half showed itself in the darkness.

Princess Landing Stage at Liverpool received us. We could feel Dad's joy at stepping ashore in England. In his exhilaration he signalled a hansom cab (much more expensive than a taxi). The cabbie in heaving our paper mache suitcases onto the roof miscalculated, causing Eddie's to be impaled on the empty whip holder. In his joy at being home father made a joke of this.

Like our Irish fellow-passengers we too began with a pilgrimage. It was to the growing-up place of father's lay hero, Lloyd George. So to Criccieth, in North Wales, between the mountains and the sea, as it featured in the great man's lilting rhetoric. From there we could walk the mile or so to Llanystumdwy, a picture-postcard village, to view the tiny house that had been the boyhood home provided by Richard Lloyd the cobbler uncle, an Old Testament figure of bearded sagacity and near-sainthood, a lay preacher of great local respect. Standing in the tiny sitting-room Father told us how the former Prime Minister and architect of post-Versailles Europe had said 'I used to think this was the largest room in the world'. Then on to the village school where the quicksilver intelligence and adroitness had been formed; my brother and I found the most impressive thing to be the primitiveness of

19   Sydney and Edward in front of Lloyd George's boyhood home, Llanystumdwy, near Criccieth, North Wales, 1928.

the outdoor lavatories. On the stone bridge over the stream immortality had been sought by the young David in boyhood fashion by carving his initials. Alas, father could not find them; time seemed already to have done its obliteration. Finally to the Village Institute. Father as an earnest young Liberal had presented to it an enlarged photograph of Richard Lloyd: it being Sunday we could not gain entry, but by peering through the windows we found it in the committee room, with its little plaque recording the donor's name. In the evening while walking about Criccieth father pointed out to us a stout little lady issuing from chapel, looking to us like Queen Victoria. This was Dame Margaret Lloyd George who, as the daughter of a local family of some substance, had married the young solicitor of humble origins. Was her decision not to live in London caused by, or the cause of his amorous escapades of which father and most of the world knew nothing? Father told us with relish how Lloyd George had defeated the local English Tory squire for the parliamentary seat of Caernarvon Boroughs. But Lloyd George had been ejected from the Prime Ministership six years earlier; he was at this moment struggling for a Liberal revival, producing a range of policies culminating in the challenging Liberal 'yellow book',

Britain's Industrial Future. Its proposals might have regenerated Britain, but this was not to be. In the General Election of 1929 the Liberals were reduced to a rump of 59 MPs, with Lloyd George, aged 66, a spent force.

From the sea coast and hills of North Wales, places of beauty which the industrial revolution had passed by and where the ancient Celtic language was still strong, we travelled by train to Birmingham. 'There you are, boys', said father, indicating the carriage window, 'a moving picture frame!' It contained the fields, the trees and hedgerows, the farmsteads, the cattle, the sheep and the horses, all set in the general greenness of England, so different from the brown of summer in Canada. There were glimpses of those corrugations of the soil that marked the ploughing with oxen of the village strips by our forebears, the medieval villeins. Approaching Birmingham we passed through the Black Country with its smoke and dirt, its slag heaps, its polluted streams from which all life had long departed, together with its factories and workshops and rows of close-packed tiny brick houses whose redness was toned to brown with smoke. Interspersed were the pubs relieving a little of the dinginess. The churches marked the presence of the established Church of England, often in sooty nineteenth century Gothic, homes of priesthood and liturgy. The chapels were scattered about in angular simplicity, small citadels of dissent where the individual stood naked before his God, scripture in hand. It was to this strand that we belonged.

Our base in Birmingham was the home of father's brother James, two years older than he. James had continued in the family tradition of the grocery trade that Dad had so loathed. He was a stout, bald headed and warm-hearted man, with large-knuckled red hands, a wizard with the bacon slicer, highly skilled in wrapping in paper, in scooping and measuring and in tying with string, an exemplar of those skills that were to be lost with the packaging revolution. He was too soft-hearted for his business, for he was haunted by the credit he had extended to those pleading for time. His wife hated the grocery trade, partly because of the strains it imposed on her husband, and partly because of its social inferiority. In spite of her distaste for her husband's business the bay window of her sitting room featured Windsor Castle modelled in Pear's soap, a former window display from the shop. She also disparaged Uncle James's deep involvement with the Disciples of Christ, of which he was a pillar. Donald and Doris their children were adults, Donald already a bowler-hatted and umbrella carrying accountant at twenty-one, working for a pair of aged partners in a Dickensian office in the heart of Birmingham; a warren and a fire trap. Though already pin-striped in body and in mind, he had a sly wit and a certain cynicism which he exercised on his uncles and aunts, enjoying making comments on them to my brother and I that were curiously illuminating. The family with James at its head was a happy one, but confined in its horizons by the financial limitations of a modest grocery store, and by the narrowing of outlook that can so easily enclose those whose lives have no discontinuities.

Uncle James took the three of us on a tour of our other Birmingham uncles. Down the road there was Uncle Wilfred the eldest, known in the family as 'The Boss'. He, who had made our Dad an uncle at birth, was now a patriarchal figure, bearded and corpulent like Edward VII. He was a user of *eau de cologne*, snuff and colourful bandana handkerchiefs, but with a weak bladder that made it necessary for Donald, who took him for walks, to calculate distances to a nicety. He had sold his six shops on good terms to a chain, including the one in Broad Street, Birmingham, over which he and his siblings had been born. We were repelled by the sombre still life in oil, featuring a brace of dead pheasants, that hung over where he sat. It was somehow inconsistent with the two chirping canaries of which he was so fond. Eddie and I were much impressed with the snuff and the explosive sneezing it induced, and by Uncle Wilfred's gesture of emptying the silver from his purse onto the table and dividing it in one sweeping gesture between us. At the other end of the scale of business success was Uncle George. He was an ageing widower with a dispirited moustache who travelled in gravy salts: the top of the bureau in his boarding house room held an ominous array of bottles. Uncle John, another grocer, we hailed from a passing bus: he and father standing at the bus stop tried to reach each other across the gulf of divergent interests and the years. Uncle Alfred, a grocer too, we found on his death bed, his waxen face partly raised by his pillows. From the background we gazed with immense respect at the wasted man, half looking forward to the awful journey we had heard so often dilated upon in church. He tried to talk to father and James, but there was the recurring refrain, 'I won't be sorry to go ...' Finally there was Uncle Walter George, relict of father's sister Mary. We had been told that he was a spiritualist, a baffling piece of information with spooky overtones. He turned out to be a crisp and businesslike man, well dressed in a nononsense fashion, who understanding boys, presented each of us with a pocket knife. When the conversation languished, as it was always in danger of doing in this series of meetings, father and Uncle Walter had a brief exchange on the subject of spiritualism. Father regarded it as not far from witchcraft, the road to madness, but managed to confine himself to a carefully controlled critique; Uncle George embarked briskly on the scientific claims of spiritualism, referring to

Sir Oliver Lodge and Sir Arthur Conan Doyle. We wondered if Uncle George was in touch with Aunt Mary, but did not dare to ask.

At the end of the tour of our senior male relations we felt how remote they were from us. Indeed we sensed that, except for James, they now meant little to father, to whom in spite of a shared home and parentage, they were strangers. We were later to learn from his conversation that this realisation had saddened him. Anecdotes about his brothers would surface in a wistful way, as for example when Uncle Wilfred in his prime would go round his shops, gather up the bits of string cut from parcels, make a heap of them on the counter, and give the newest employee a lecture on the importance of small economies.

With Aunts Ellen and Louise it was different. They had brought father up after his mother had died when he was eight. Ellen had been pretty; she had enjoyed her marriage and still sorely missed married life even some twenty years after her husband's death. Father believed that I looked like her, a thought that disturbed me because she had lost all her upper incisors except one, which our cousin Donald wickedly called her pickled onion chaser. Her hands had become knobbly, but were renowned in the family for the quantities of lace they had produced in their fight against arthritis. She could still play the piano in her simple way; rendering hymns with special pathos, 'Steal away, steal away to Jesus'. Louise was a tiny creature who held things together, accepting her sister's whims as the only way to protect her; she had received one proposal of marriage from a commercial representative over the counter in James's shop where she worked, but as he was not one of the Disciples, after much searching of her heart she had sent him away. It was Louise who had worried over father as he, the bright one of the family, had gone through the crises of adolescence and young manhood; she had been, in a sense, his surrogate mother.

This Martha and Mary pair of aunts lived in a small brick terrace house with a little yard at the rear that was largely taken up by an outside lavatory and a large wooden roller mangle. The sitting room was a crowded place with heavy drapes on the single window fringed with tassels; the piano had candle holders, with antimacassars on the chairs. Father sat amid the Victorian and Edwardian relics that populated the room, just as he had done when he was a rebellious clerk in the Shropshire Union Canal Company. As I was to realise years later, this was the most intimate glimpse we were ever to have of father's past. Even a conversation held in the street with his former fiancée, still a spinster, who had jilted him all those years ago, made no such impact, for we boys did not really know who she was until much later and so did not attune ourselves to the nuances.

20   Edward, Sydney and their father in Moseley Park, Birmingham, Summer
1928.

A major concern of father's was to introduce us to real cricket and
real football. Cricket was the halcyon sport for him, the essence of the
England he had lost, where the chivalry of sportsmanship met the rule
of law in the unquestioned authority of the umpire. Each batsman
walked to his crease and was there tested against eleven opponents
under the open sky. The crowd was silent while each ball was bowled,
and then applauded the play rather than the side. With all of this went
telling phrases, 'facing the bowling', 'keeping a straight bat', 'knocking
for six' and 'the game's the thing'. Father spoke with affectionate awe
of the cricketers he had watched including Prince Ranji, 'like a great
cat about the wicket', and the mighty Jack Hobbs, a 'player' who knew
his place in life among the 'gentlemen', but who had the dignity of a
master of his craft. Against all this father posed the raucous par-
tisanship of American baseball and its razzing of the umpire. He took
us to the Warwickshire County Cricket ground at Edgbaston to demonstrate the nature of cricket. It was as he had said, full of leisurely
decorum and connoisseurship of play. But to our eyes, North Amer-
icanised as they were, and ignorant of the finer points, there was
insufficient action. Moreover to our intense embarrassment, father had
done himself up in a blazer and a shapeless white hat of a generation

earlier. It required the reflection of later years to sense what he felt and his bafflement that he could not arouse the same feeling for cricket in us.

He suffered a like frustration with soccer. Of this too he was an enthusiast, eager to join a lower order of society than the patrons of cricket, ready to bellow at the players from among the cloth capped workmen in the stands in support of Aston Villa, yet still acclaiming good play and respecting the referee. But commercialism had intruded much further into soccer than into cricket by 1928: the game he took us to was far more brutal than he had remembered. This he did not realise while the match was on, for he was carried away purple-faced in his support of the team of his youth. Later, however, his indignation at the debasement of the game began to surface, especially when he described it to James.

Westward we went to Clifton and Bristol to see mother's people. Brunel's bridge gracefully suspended on its cables high over the dramatic Avon Gorge and swaying slightly underfoot, epitomised Clifton for us as the place where mother had grown up. High on a bluff nearby was the *camera obscura*, throwing on its great circular table an image of the scene around both far and near: it discovered a courting couple all unawares on a bench, but disappointed us by moving discreetly on.

Aunt Evelyn, mother's sister, who still looked astonishingly like her, gave us tea. She and her husband Uncle Angus had lived for a time in Winnipeg: there was a family legend that they had awakened one night to find an Indian leaning over the bed, his face a few inches from theirs. Uncle Angus for some years, we gathered, had been showing signs of peculiarity, especially in the direction of miserliness and in a taste for the macabre. Not long before, walking on the downs, he had found a man on a park bench with his throat cut: he gave us an irrepressible account of this encounter. He sat in an ancient armchair, the padding of which had come through the upholstery at various places. Having a running nose he had festooned used handkerchiefs along both arms of his chair; these he blew into in a clockwise sequence, carefully spreading each to dry. He had contracted his cold the previous Saturday at the nearby seaside resort of Weston-super-mare. A national newspaper in low water, the *Westminster Gazette*, had hit upon the imaginative circulation-boosting device of planting on the promenade of a chosen resort each Saturday a man of the most ordinary appearance, calling him Lobby Lud, having the previous day published his photograph; members of the public were invited to carry a copy of the newspaper, as did Mr. Lud, and, for a prize of £50, to identify him, pronouncing the words: 'You are Mr. Lobby Lud and I claim the *Westminster Gazette* prize!' Uncle Angus, dubbed by us 'Uncle

Moses', had trudged about for a rain-sodden day peering into men's faces and catching his cold.

Millie was mother's favourite cousin: she had not married, but lived in the semi-basement of the boarding house by which she kept herself and her ancient father. He sat by the fire, burning brightly in this semi-subterranean setting on a hot August afternoon. He had been 'in service' all his life, rising to the status of butler in a large country house. When he was a lad Charles Dickens had given him a shilling to go skating on the Serpentine. One of his periods of service had been in France, causing him to say at intervals to father, 'I can speak French, you know'. He failed to give us a demonstration.

London, of course, was the greatest centrepiece of our travels. For father it was, as in his youth, the Imperial city, a place at which to marvel. He took great pride in his ability to lead us from one landmark to another. We did all the sights, but somehow always seemed to return to Whitehall and Westminster from where Britain and the Empire were governed. The Cenotaph in Whitehall was then still new, as was the feeling of the national loss: when a bus load of men passed it many of them would raise their hats to the fallen. Whitehall was the ground trodden by the men of destiny. In the Abbey he had little to say about its medieval glories; Poets' Corner was rather better, but it was to the statues of statesmen that he warmed. It was the same at Madame Tussauds: he offered to identify the effigies of the great men, with us to check him against the catalogue. He impressed us greatly, except for one debacle. In the section on Imperial Statesmen we stood in front of a shortish figure with a shock of red hair. Father was baffled and annoyed while we giggled. This was Madame's quite unrealistic rendering of Mackenzie King. Next to the statesmen for father ranked the prose writers: he was much drawn to the men who by the use of words had made themselves immortal. We had lunch in the *Cheshire Cheese* off Fleet Street, an expensive departure from Lyons standardised eating places. Father showed us where the giants of Grubb Street, Dr. Johnson, Dickens, Chesterton and others had sat in their respective eras; he conjured up for us 'the great lexicographer' responding to Boswell, each gem introduced with the magisterial 'Sir, ...'

But father had of course no entrée to the great private interiors. The National Liberal Club, the shrine of Liberalism, with its statues and portraits of Gladstone, Lloyd George, Asquith and the rest of the political pantheon of his youth, was closed to him. So too was the clubland of St. James, though he pointed out the Reform Club where Jules Verne's hero Phineas Fogg had made the bet that propelled him round the world in eighty days. The great houses of the Mall and of Regents Park were a world unimaginably remote. So too was that of the

Bloomsbury group, with their corrosive influence on the England father cherished in his heart. Nor did he have any acquaintance with the dense slumland of London's East End, or with the beginnings of attempts to alleviate it by the construction of council estates around the perimeter of the city. His was a London encapsulated in space and time, confined to its central parts where there was a drama and high human expression, most of it associated with a past that was as real as ever to father, but which was fading in the minds of the Londoners themselves, separated from father's England by the bitterness of the General Strike only two years before.

While we were crossing the Horse Guards Parade Dad broke into a run. He overtook a tiny man, aged but sprightly, in a blue serge suit and bowler hat. This was the Rt. Hon. John Burns, one of the two members of the British Cabinet who had resigned on the declaration of war in Germany in 1914. Father engaged him in conversation. On learning we were Canadians Mr. Burns pronounced: 'You Canadians were fooled into the war. It was nothing but a King's family row!' Father, though silently disagreeing, was delighted with this unequivocal pronouncement. It has always returned to me as a warning example of the simplistic perspectives that can guide even men of power.

On the staff of the *Daily Mail* was Karl Ketchum, who had begun as a reporter in Ottawa, and who now had some claim to be the most travelled newspaperman in Britain. We went to see him. He greeted us expansively, indulging himself as one of the great men of Fleet Street. But foreign assignments had begun to bore him. He propositioned father to go to Paris to cover that Peace Conference out of which came the Kellogg Pact. Perhaps he wanted to give him a glimpse of the big-time. Dad declined.

Two spectacles made a deep impression on us. There was the changing of the guard at Buckingham Palace, by the Household Cavalry in Whitehall. Here were men immaculately resplendent in the trappings of pre-industrial war, following patterns of total discipline and absolute excellence within an archaic formula. The other was the traffic control by the Metropolitan Police before the age of traffic lights. Teams of Bobbies stood at the great confluences of traffic, like Piccadilly, with their majestic white-gauntleted gestures, manipulating by judgement and force of will the mighty surges of vehicles. Ottawa, even at the corner of Bank and Sparks, had nothing like this!

To see so much of Britain so quickly we had to spend a lot of time in trains. In 1928 the Flying Scotsman began its non-stop runs from King's Cross to Edinburgh, a kind of final crowning glory of British railway achievement. It was steam of course, with the characteristic sulphurous soot and cinders that struck the face and lodged in the eyes if you disobeyed the signs and stuck your head out of the windows. Passengers accepted their quota of smut on face, hands and clothing. The great vaults of girders and glass of the major stations were impregnated with the same coal-burning smell. There were glimpses of dignified stationmasters in top hats and frock coats whose watches were drawn forth on their chains to check that departures and arrivals were on the very stroke. The guard with his whistle and green flag was a military figure, smartly turned out, with a sense of his own authority. The smaller stations were resplendent in their bright upkeep, with freshly painted signs, and carefully tended flowerbeds, with the name of the station picked out in bright whitewashed stones or even variegated plants, with no scrap of rubbish in sight. British trains, with their diminutive engines, pulled smoothly out of the station with a gentle chuff-chuff so different from the clanging and jerking of Canadian trains. Moreover you could step into them at platform level rather than mounting a set of steep steps. The tiny freight wagons, seemed hardly big enough to merit loading and unloading.

From the train you could see a lot of England and Scotland that was not otherwise visible. The iron foundries, engineering works, steel mills, and scrapyards with their chimneys and waste heaps were symbols of the heavy metal base of Victorian industrialisation, beginning to be pervaded with the rust of obsolescence. City houses along the railway line showed their fronts to the street, asserting their privacy in the English fashion, but their backs lay open to the view of the railway passenger. There were side by side gardens cultivated with pride and back yards that were mere receptacles for the family junk. Sometimes the pub was the only building with any sign of prosperity. Clear of the towns the countryside would yield a glimpse of an ancient church, the banner of St. George fluttering from its tower, the focus of the kind of village from which the urban masses had come. Distantly there might be a country house among its trees, the scene of graceful living on the basis of cheap labour, where the landed culture that had bred Governors-General for Canada like Bessborough and Willingdon was living out its last phase.

Our longest train journey carried us to Edinburgh. At York Station father sought tea from a trolley on the platform. The guard blew his whistle just as father had picked up his three cups: we watched with queasy fascination as he tottered toward the train as the guard moved along the platform slamming the doors, knowing that tickets, money, addresses and indeed all that documented and financed our existence was in his pocket. He sat down in triumph, perspiring heavily, the three saucers awash and the cups half empty. Not long after two genial gentlemen entered our carriage and produced a pack of cards. Being

21   Edward and Sydney in front of the Forth Railway Bridge, Summer 1928.

professional sharpers working the trains they soon saw that father and the other gent present offered no prospects. The expanse of the Yorkshire Moors seen from the train window reminded me of how we had been taught that England was a land of crowded cities.

Father revelled in Edinburgh, with its grey stone buildings heaped up to the crowning glory of its Castle. This was the land of John Knox who could carry through a purging of the nation almost single handed (and whose house was to be seen in the High Street). The land of Covenanting zeal inspired dedicated men meeting in secret for the faith (whose place of execution could be seen in the Grassmarket) the land of great preachers who admonished the people (whose pulpits stood in St. Giles Cathedral and in the graceful Georgian churches of the New Town), and of brave fighting men (whose National Memorial was to be visited in the Castle). We climbed Calton Hill to look down on Princes Street, the Scott Monument and indeed the whole splendid scene, the air impregnated with the distinctive smell of the breweries. We journeyed by char-a-banc to view the engineering wonder of the world, the Forth Bridge, with father instructing us on the cantilever principle that made possible the massive structure. Viewed obliquely it looked like the skeleton of some great three-humped monster.

22   Sydney and Edward at York Minster, Summer 1928.

We returned for a final visit to Birmingham via York. We walked
about the great Minster and looked down upon the ancient city from
its roof leads and crocketed pinnacles. In the teashop opposite the West
door we saw father covertly looking into his wallet as he changed one
of those splendid fold-out five pound notes which looked as though the
Governor of the Bank of England had signed it himself. We sensed that
breaking into a fiver was one of those landmarks on the financial road,
and that father was calculating whether he had enough money to see
us through. As we were approaching the end of our visit to England,
and uplifted by the glories of York Minster, he had tried once more to
elicit from us some reaction to all that we had seen. But we shared his
perversity (and fear of sentimentality). We simply could not respond.
I had, however, evolved a formula for meeting father's approaches,
describing each of the sights that had secretly stirred me as 'Fair'. I

think he understood. I hope so. I sympathise now how it was that Dr. Johnson in his advanced years could journey to his hometown of Litchfield and stand for a day in the town square in a kind of penance for all that he might have said to his father when he had the chance.

Those eight intense weeks were to leave an abiding mark on my inner self, providing an anthology of recollection to be drawn upon throughout the rest of my life. There is in the mind a kind of encapsulated England which all the subsequent changes seem only to have heightened in memory. This was the England of so many tiny houses, often indeed in continuous terraces with vanishing perspectives, with dark linoleum covered corridors and remote kitchens overlooking dingy little courtyards, houses never wholly heated either by summer sun or winter fireplaces. Yet their rooflines were dominated by chimneys and chimney pots, their stone and brick walls were streaked with soot. Their plumbing hung outside like varicose veins. Slightly grander terraces like cousin Millie's had their front steps beneath which were semi-basements, with back gardens defined by brick walls often topped with cemented broken glass. The pubs punctuated the streets, centres of communal life or dens of vice as you might choose to view them. Old ladies were old ladies, their sexual urges assumed to have ceased at menopause, long since interred under sombre clothes. The boys wore stove-pipe pants and school caps of various degrees of decrepitude, finding our knickerbockers hilarious. The King, the little bearded sailor with his trousers pressed down the sides in the nautical manner, was held in universal affection. There was the ginger beer in stone bottles and a preference for tinned condensed milk rather than fresh. It was an England where they did indeed shout 'Owzatt?' to the cricket umpire and where the glamour-men of the soccer pitches, the heroes of the terraces (stands), wore brilliant white cotton 'shorts' that reached from mid-knee to mid navel, their immense bagginess covering a distance greater than that from navel to neck and so wholly free from eroticism. The effect was completed by oiled centre hairpartings and short back and sides. This was the England between the crisis of the General Strike and when the roof fell in with the Great Depression of the 1930s. England was still culturally itself, with no visible sign of American influence except for the burgeoning cinemas. But the Channel had in a sense disappeared, for as Dad pointed out to us, Mr. Baldwin announced to the public while we were there that London was indefensible from the air.

On the sea journey home father was terribly sick, so much so as to frighten us. Perhaps he finally knew that the England he had loved was slipping away, that the Old Country, that land of afternoon, that retreat within the head, was vanishing. He had bought himself a new frock coat to wear to church; being fearful that the customsmen would charge him for it, he wore it to go ashore in Montreal. We returned to Britannia in a mood of triumph, to discover that we immediately fitted back into context, and that no one except mother was particularly interested to hear of our adventures.

There was a year to go before High School. In it father finally abandoned his high starched collars and his gold watch chain. The links of the latter had become very thin: father refused the suggestion that he should have it melted down and remade. 'You could never be sure you would get the same gold back', he said. This would mean that he would no longer have the gift from his sisters that had marked his twenty-first birthday. The watch chain went into his drawer along with the carton of abandoned collars.

CHAPTER 9

High School

I entered my teens on 9 October 1929. Before the month was out came the Wall Street crash, the harbinger of the world's greatest depression. A few weeks earlier I had become a High School student at Lisgar Collegiate Institute where my older brother was a veteran of one year's standing. For those gamblers on the stock exchange who had lost all, father had no sympathy: he liked to recount the behaviour of the dentist who kept trotting from his chair to the phone to check on the slide of his International Nickel shares, a favourite Ottawa speculation.

High School was a world in which our parents could have no part. Their education had ended when they were twelve or thirteen, the age at which this second and critical phase of ours began. For them there had been no algebra, geometry, physics or botany, French or Latin. Indeed it was to become a mischievous pleasure to take home the textbooks that contained these mysteries and display acquaintance with them.

Life for boys at Lisgar Collegiate began in Middle Earth, the boys' basement. Its great figure was a terrifying man the janitor. He had been a sergeant-major in the British army, with service in Kipling's India, Egypt, South Africa and France. Now approaching sixty he was a fearsome sight for a nervous boy entering upon the proto-adulthood of high school life. His enormous belly could fill one of the urinals as in leisurely fashion he relieved himself, his elbows spread along the tops of the adjacent conveniences. Under the peak of his cap (spirit-level straight with regimental severity) were brooding eyes, continually on the watch for breaches of discipline among the smaller boys. Further down was a wide-wingspan waxed moustache in the Kitchener mode, with great spiked ends. It served as an external indicator of his internal mood: if its points were properly horizontal there was a good chance that his choler was under the control of his will. If they were awry, one end up and the other down, this was a danger warning. From his belt hung a vast bunch of keys, symbols of mysterious custodianships. At his heels there was usually one or more of the Airedale dogs which he bred under circumstances unimaginable to us. When in English

103

classes we reached Falstaff he took the janitorial shape, though we could not imagine him babbling of green fields, he being never seen other than in Middle Earth.

The boys' basement was a place of distilled maledom and total philistinism. Its concrete floors, labyrinths of lockers, closeness to the gym, urinals and lavatories, furnished a world of distinctive ethos, some of it derived from the wider adult male world, some of it peculiar to the ages of 13 to 18. There was the gymnasium dressing room with its massage table of independently springy boards which could badly pinch your tender parts. After the shower room, where there was much playful flicking of towels by older boys at the private parts of friends, came the boys' gym. The whole was permeated with the smells of sweat, disinfectant, linament, urinals, and the dreadful Airedales, together with the concentrated odour of hundreds of boys.

The school coach, Dutch Brulard, assigned the lockers. The larger ones near the dressing room were awarded to the heroes of the school teams. These were ostentatiously full of sweatshirts with the school crest, skates, shoulderpads, jock straps, basketball shoes (trade name *Fleet Foot*) and unwashed towels that stiffened like corpses when they dried. There was a communalism of soap, towels, sweaters, combs and the like, but within circles of friendship.

Coach and janitor were the rival dieties of this *nieblungen* world, fearful presences to be avoided and observed from afar by a timid twelve-year old of less than one hundred pounds. But the two gods, though wary and formal with one another, did not clash. For by an instinctive adjustment the boy denizens of Middle Earth observed two jurisdictions, the one when young and the other when comfortably up the school. For though the janitor could terrorise the smaller boys with his parade-ground roar, the senior boys took him as a figure of fun, though never to his face. Their allegiance was to Brulard who picked the teams, the recognised accolade. Boys in their final year, if they were representing the school, especially in the more gladatorial sports, were the recognised heroes. They moved about the basement with muscular serenity, aware that they were superior beings among males and that they had a potent effect upon females. Even they, however, did not wholly escape from Higgins' orbit, for he had set up a small business of selling doughnuts and glasses of milk from a table under the stairs to which boys of all ages, permanently hungry, had recourse.

The Principal never penetrated to these nether regions, nor did the teachers: Higgins and Brulard were the sole adults. That is, except for Bob Scarfe, Higgins' assistant who, like so many in a secondary role, performed most of the duties of his superior, in his case doing all those things necessary to keep the central heating and other services going.

Only when there was an important basketball game in the gym were the girls permitted to pass through the basement. The knowledgeable among them knew that they must turn sharp right at the bottom of the stairs, for to the left were the urinals in full view. They then passed the open dressing room door with averted gaze to arrive demurely on the narrow gallery of the gym, bringing with them the odour and aura of another world. On one occasion a pair of nuns attending a teaching demonstration in the school had wandered down a flight too many and had turned left. The boys were thrown into a catatonic confusion at these so alien bodies, but Mr. Higgins, with the command of situations gained on so many imperial parade grounds behind him, escorted these incarnations of innocence away from the danger of exposure to male functions.

At nine o'clock each morning Mr. Higgins ceremoniously undid the padlock which secured the folding gate half way up the stairs leading to the school proper. With the gates pushed to each side he would turn and descend slowly to his own realm, his vast stomach like the prow of a galleon dividing the upward surge of boys moving to where there were teachers and girls.

For a new boy fighting his way upward to a larger and brighter world for the first time these were indeed the two challenges awaiting him, namely teachers and girls. That of the teachers had to be responded to first. For the teachers were the source of authority, of rewards and punishments. Contact had to be made at once with them, for in contrast to the girls, there was no take-it-or-leave-it option.

Morning Assembly was the place where the whole school, apart from the rulers of the basement, was set out to view. From the back seats of the gallery where the first formers sat there was a panorama of this new world. The Principal took his place on the stage in a kind of grandeur while the Assistant Principal saw that things went smoothly. The Principal seemed a diety far eclipsing the now dimmed presences of the basement, for we had not yet been told by the rougher boys that he stood at the bottom of the stairs when classes were changing in order the better to look up the girls' skirts. At the appropriate moment the Principal pronounced the words of welcome to us newcomers in a form we were to become accustomed to in subsequent years. There were mildly inspirational references to the school's spirit and its achievements.

Assembly began with the Lord's Prayer and a short Bible reading, chosen so as not to offend Christian sectarians or Jews, the product of some distant compromise between secular and religious education. The Canadian flag was nowhere to be seen: far from pledging the flag in the American school fashion we scarcely knew it. A feature of

Assembly was the singing led by Dr. Bearder, a Pinnochio of a man with a button nose and a great belief in the educational value of community singing. The words of what we were to sing were thrown on a screen by magic lantern and the melody was rendered by the school orchestra consisting for the most part of the more studious students; none of the males among them had large lockers. Dr. Bearder's choice of songs was highly idiosyncratic: why, for example, were we celebrating Mother Macrae:

> *I'm a long way from home*
> *And my thoughts ever roam*
> *To old Erin far over the sea ...*

For the older teachers the arrival of a new set of first-form kids was part of their annual cycle, part of life's routine. Each met it in his or her established style. There were those who began with an assertion of iron authority, not to say terror. There was the aged Liz Thomson, the ear-twister. We were soon to learn her methods, combining fierce ironic tongue with this form of physical assault that put no strain on her ancient physique. To every class from the outset she posed a fearful gamble. 'Those who have not done their homework', she would say with quiet menace, 'will stand up'. Only the most reckless or fearless, or the possessors of the toughest ears, would take the risk of being caught out. Less subtle was Mr. Stenten, a short but very powerful man in his fifties with heavy jowls. Hardly had we sat down in his classroom, fearfully recalling the relished tales told by elder brothers, when he suddenly and apparently quite unaccountably, threw down the vast wooden ruler he used for drawing geometric diagrams on the blackboard, strode to the rear of the class where experience told him the tougher boys would sit, seized the largest, icily told him to remove his glasses, hauled him into the aisle and shook him until both ears were purple, dumping him back into his seat. Teachers such as these acted from the outset to get their message of mastery across. Beginning in this way they were secure in their control over the generations, able in the upper classes, if they were so disposed, to mellow from strength, allowing glimpses of humanity to peak through, thus compounding their legend and sticking in the minds of their pupils for the rest of their lives.

At the opposite extreme was the Scot, Mr. Neilson and others like him. He was a gentle, whispish man who had for decades hoped to carry young male barbarians and the girls to whom they displayed along on the glories of English literature. After only a class or two on *The Merchant of Venice* Mr. Neilson's delicate interpretation of Shylock and his place in the life of Venice, including his association with Tubal a brother money-lender, the cry kept coming from the back of the class: 'Sir, tell us more about Two-ball. We want to hear about Two-ball'. But Mr. Neilson persevered, bearing his cross daily, indeed hourly. Not so Mr. Plimmon. He was in the last stages of disintegration. In him we caught our first sight of a man demoralised to the point of breakdown. He was to be relentlessly thrust from his profession by a section of the male young who, sensing weakness, followed the atavistic instinct of the hunter in for the kill. Though high school boys were not yet prepared to challenge the entire system, they were ready to destroy individuals, impelled by male assertion.

Against those who held their ground by fear and those who lost it by timorousness must be placed those teachers who by their strength of character had no need to think of discipline. Jennie Murray, head of modern languages and teacher of French, was such. She was a matronly looking spinster of around fifty, with a presence that was a warning that deterred all triflers. Her pince-nez was on a long, fine gold chain which, after a slight tug would coil quickly into its small container the size and shape of an overcoat button pinned to her ample bosom. Occasionally she would catch the chain on some part of her person, activating the spring so that the glasses would suddenly be snatched from her nose. No one laughed. Even when, having set a brief assignment, she left the room and the lavatory in the women teachers' rest room was shortly afterward completing its evacuation, filling her classroom with a sound she knew not of, she could return with her composure undisturbed by any ribaldry among the class. She regularly visited France. She obtained the latest aids for the teaching of French and displayed them to her classes in which impervious Anglo-Scottish children were the largest element. There were gramophone records of the company of the *Comedie Française* doing Molière's *L'Avare*: it was a thrill one could not confess to, hearing a marvellous base-baritone voice playing the part of the miser bemoaning the theft of his hoard, especially the line *'Je suis mort, je suis enterre!'* Around the walls of the room on two sides above the blackboards were blown-up photographs of French mouths demonstrating the positions of tongue, teeth and epiglottis for making the correct sounds. For Miss Murray correct speech and an appreciation of high literature were the ends to be sought, rather than the kind of simple conversation that would have allowed us to talk to people over the river in Hull, in French speaking Quebec. Perhaps she thought such speech was degenerate, lacking the discipline imposed by the *Academie Française*. On the other hand each class began with her entrance, followed by the class saying in unison, *'Bonjour, Mademoiselle'*, with her replying in full formality,

'Bonjour mes élèves'. There were faint signs of spinsterish obsession: waste paper should never be crumpled for the basket, but neatly torn once across the middle: the rationale of this was that the basket did not fill so quickly.

Two teachers of English enjoyed high esteem. There was 'Hank' Stann, perhaps nicknamed because of the hanks of hair he diligently spread across his scalp from its right sideline. He was a man from whom emanated simultaneously a friendly interest and a deep menace, the latter of the oral kind. 'What mark did you expect for this piece of work?' he asked a pupil. 'Very little, sir', was the reply. 'Blessed is he that expecteth nothing', said Hank in a quietly reflective voice that filled the room, 'For he shall not be disappointed when he receiveth the same'.

But it was Jimmie Dunlop, another Scot, a small man with a fine grey face and a quiet manner, who could bring life out of the textbook classics. He would ask a member of the class to read a passage. This would be done in the flat embarrassed tones of youth. Mr. Dunlap would then read it again himself, sometimes interspersing explanation, so that meaning would be lifted from the page. There was in him a real though muted histrionic gift, which when mixed with his scholarly sense of the text, produced a deep impression. He knew Scotland and England and loved them, and he had served in France. One 11th November he laid down the textbook and recited to us in his quiet voice:

> *I saw the spires of Oxford*
> *As I was passing by*
> *The grey spires of Oxford*
> *Against a pearl-grey sky*
> *And my heart was with the Oxford men*
> *Who went abroad to die.*

In another mood he could be gently mocking, as for example when discussing chivalry as depicted by Sir Walter Scott. But in spite of his throw-away and deprecatory manner he was the kind of man who would have answered Roland's horn had it called him, perhaps a little wearily and with a shrug. In one of his asides addressed to himself as much as us he once said: 'The man who is afraid to be alone with himself is incomplete'.

On the science side there was Old Bill Beaton and Fussy Irvine. Old Bill was a dour Scot from Glasgow who seemed to live a kind of inward life, even when he was conducting experiments for us in physics and chemistry. Even this however was preferable to the introspective mood which made him say on entering the classroom: 'Tak' doon these problems', after which he would assume a Buddha-like silence seated at the laboratory desk staring vacantly over our bowed heads. But even his banked fires could burst forth. One afternoon when an experiment failed to produce the predicted result a voice from the back of the class hissed 'Fake!' Old Bill marched unerringly to the back of the room, seized the hisser and propelled him up the aisle and into the corridor where there ensued an impressive dressing-down. Antithetical to Old Bill was Fussy Irvine. He seemed to exist in a permanent aura of hydrogen sulphide. He was an overt enthusiast for science and for communicating it. One morning in 1932 he arrived with the newspaper in his hand: it contained an account of the splitting of the atom by Cockcroft. He recounted to us this new marvel of science in a mixture of reverence and excitement. Here was the potential for a new and unlimited source of power for mankind. 'A cup of water', said Fussy, 'will power the greatest liner across the Atlantic'.

For the most part those who taught us were real teachers. They accepted full responsibility for our education. They did not expect parents to stand over their kids while they did their homework; instead they applied their own sanctions. They took it to be part of their job to inculcate the ethic of hard work. Examinations were accepted by teachers and taught alike as something ordained and immutable, against which we had to be measured, rather like an anticipation of the Last Judgement. Conversely our teachers did not expect to be required to do our parents' job: the idea of the 'pastoral' approach in which they sorted out the children's lives did not enter their heads: this was the responsibility of parents, Sunday Schools and churches.

The clear implication of the work ethic was that those who failed could only blame themselves. Similarly with false values: it was with secret self-satisfaction that we saw those flashy princes in *The Merchant of Venice* choose the wrong caskets. We learned too that the Persians had been a corrupt and voluptuous lot, the purveyors of nameless sins from the east, whose vast armies could be stopped by a handful of Greeks with the right values (which in some vague sense were ours). As in church, so in school, moral judgements were pervasive. Rather than inquire why certain people or peoples behaved in certain ways, we were taught to place them against a scale of approval and disapproval. The day of moral relativism had not yet dawned.

Each teacher had a fixed syllabus to cover, especially in mathematics and the sciences. Learning had been parcelled out in an orderly fashion between teachers and classes, each 'subject' of which served as an examination for the appropriate age group. In most cases there was a brisk start, with little by way of preliminary. Geometry was a preeminent example. We were told what axioms are, namely the self-evident propositions on which all else is based. Theorem One followed at once, plunging us into the angles at the base of an isosceles triangle. From the outset there was a strict mode for writing up laboratory experiments (object, equipment, experiment, observation, conclusion). This was intended to inculcate the scientific mode of thinking, demonstrating that the same set of circumstances will always produce the same results. In short we learned that we lived in a strictly causal world, susceptible of being expressed mathematically. But this was never explicitly said: there was no introduction to the physical world in philosophical terms. We were not invited to share in the excitement of those who had first hit upon these things: Euclid among the Greeks, Leonardo's perception that the natural world was to be viewed in terms of process and function, Newton's astrophysics that were dynamic in showing how the heavenly bodies could move in settled paths without collision, but static in regarding the universe as a self-equilibrating clockwork. Perhaps it was the better approach to teach propositions, how they are composed and how they relate on a grander scale. Certainly there were many kids (of which I was not one) who seemed to have a natural affinity for maths and science as they were presented, perceiving without effort what a problem involved.

No link was made between our science and our religion. There was a general implication that because there was so much evidence of design (all those theorems, laws, uniformities and consistencies that bound the natural world together), there must have been a Designer (God). But there was an unresolved collision between this idea on the one hand, resting so heavily on strict causality, and on the other the suspensions of natural law in the Old Testament and the New. Had God really intervened with His creation to punish and reward the people of Israel; what of the virgin birth of Christ, His miracles, the resurrection and His assumption into heaven? Was prayer really a personal, group or communal plea for a suspension of the rules of a causal world?

Languages were treated in the main in the same didactic fashion as was science, as learning exercises. There was little concern with the cultures that had formed them or the great men who had employed them. There were some children who seemingly had the effortless knack of Latin proses, receiving them back free or almost so of Lucy Brown's blue pencil. Though my own proses were returned terribly scarred, enough of vocabulary and sentence construction remained to open the door to those 12,000 words that Latin has brought to the English language since the Renaissance, making possible greater precision of expression and more subtle shades of meaning. Even Miss

Murray, though she was the only person whom we knew who had lived in Paris, did not seek to bring France close to us as a living thing, no doubt because of the pressure of the syllabus and her daily testing of our vocabulary assignments. We did not, for example, realise that the antecedents of our French Canadians were peasants of the north-west of France, from Normandy and Britanny, endowed with the dourness and quality of enduring necessary to survive the Canadian winter, and not from the sunny southern lands of Mediterranean France where passions ran high and temperament was unstable and where the land was dotted with Roman ruins. Nor had Miss Murray time to tell us of the differences between modern France and the Kingdom of the Bourbons from which the British had seized Canada in 1759. In particular the cultural and philosophical turmoil of the France of the 1920sand early 1930s was passed over. We heard nothing of Dada and the surrealists, the flowering of jazz, the reign of Cocteau. Perhaps that grand clash between the new demand for the release of spontaneity, intuition and the unconscious, and the classical instinct for order and restraint, would have been beyond Canadian High School kids, but it might have been worth a try to convey it, had the mechanics of the language not demanded so much attention.

Only in history classes did we acquire any sense of context, of the setting within which things happened to societies and to individuals. Canadian history was ostensibly our teachers' main effort to help us to locate ourselves in time and space. It seemed to us to be a curiously anaemic affair. There were all those early explorers, whose routes across Canada had to be drawn in dotted lines, crosses or other mark-ings; there was the Conquest, with Wolfe and Montcalm sharing a chivalrous fight in which there was really no loser; there was the somewhat tepid story of Confederation, so lacking in the kind of resounding eighteenth-century declaration that American history had produced. The teaching was from a textbook published in 1928: at its conclusion it scurried through the triumphant war of 1914-18 and Canada's proud participation in the Versailles Peace Treaty, made a passing reference to the Winnipeg General Strike of 1919 and con-cluded by saying 'gradually the people of Canada have recovered from the unrest and depression of the period following the war'. The question of French Canada had been laid to rest and the east-west tensions within the Dominion, given a new intensity by the depression of the 1930s, was largely passed over, as was the curse of unemployment.

There appear to have been two subliminal objectives to this form of presentation, projected for us by the Province of Ontario. One had to do with the related problems of patriotism and reconciliation. Whereas in American schools patriotism could be pursued with single-mindedness, focussed on the flag and the pledge to it, in Canada the melting pot had not been able to render down the recalcitrant lump of the French. Our history had therefore to do its best to imply that the lily of France and the thistle of Scotland and the rose of England would

> *... entwine*
> *With the Maple leaf forever.*

The history of Canada, too bland already, was paradoxically made the more so by a fundamental fissure in Canadian society.

Then there was the projection of morality. There was a strong official and religious code. To teach morality to the young it must be possible to demonstrate or imply that it has been a powerful force in the history of one's country. Its principles must be taken to have operated in the nation's affairs and in the actions of its leaders. Too much discussion either of historical determinism or of expediency or contrivance or cheating by factions or leaders could be damaging to any elevated view of human conduct.

So it was with a kind of relief that we moved on to European history. It contained real drama—the mighty surge of events, with charismatic leaders, and with no inhibitions about describing their actions. There was Bismarck and his cynical working on German politics and on the map of Europe, the manipulator who consulted no generalised morality of the southern Ontario official kind, but who set his objectives and pursued them. Even more to taste was the French Revolution, presenting an ancient and powerful society in turmoil, incapable of a new equilibrium. There was Robespierre, the sea-green incorruptible, the absolute moralist wading through blood to impose his arbitrary puritanism; the horrific St. Just, the symbol of psychopathic violence with the ears of his enemies dangling from the brim of his hat; Danton meeting his fate with the cry 'Danton! No weakness!' The whole culminated in Napoleon, the tiny titan, passing through his incredible arc in so few years, trying to turn revolution into European hegemony and ending as a prisoner of the British on a dingy South Atlantic island. This was the stuff to stir the blood and the imagination. Beside the tumbrils of the terror the stoning of Lord Elgin's carriage in Montreal in 1849, the high point in Canadian political violence, seemed a mild affair.

We knew that the Ottawa Valley or indeed the continental scale of our Confederation had played no part in these great sweeps of history. And yet they were ours—the British heritage with its aura of power and glory belonged to us no less than to those still in England, Scotland,

Ireland and Wales. We felt we too had had a share in putting Napoleon on the deck of the *Bellerephon* to be carried into final exile, as shown in the engraved print on the classroom wall.

Would we ourselves ever be called upon to play a part in great events, to right great wrongs, to determine history? Our elders seemed to think that this was at least a possibility. Cadet training, begun at Elgin, was continued at Lisgar, presumably against such an eventuality. The corps was voluntary, though there was considerable moral pressure to join. Marching and elementary rifle drill in the gym were sometimes substituted for P.T. in the winter months. For this purpose Mr. Carter turned up. He was very different from Mr. Collins. In contrast to Mr. Collins' crisp uniform Mr. Carter wore a crumpled blue suit, making him look sadly civilian. He lacked the presence to control some fifty boys at a time, especially at rifle drill, so that there was much unauthorised stamping of rifle butts on the floor, together with non-response to orders that made chaos of the drill. In the tiny rifle range up under the rafters of the school we were taught to fire .22 calibre rifles fitted to standard army stocks. Though these were so simple, they conveyed a first fascination with weaponry, with their beautifully machined parts shining in their skin of oil, articulating against one another. Then there were the parades, culminating in June in Lansdowne Park with a march-past taken by a senior officer. The stock of uniforms, deeply wrinkled and musty, was taken out of store and distributed a few days before the great event, involving dedicated mothers in much pressing and some judicious altering. The parade itself meant marching through the streets as somewhat sheepish and untried heroes, with ancient Ross rifles on our shoulders, our shoes slipping in the tar of the sun-softened road surface.

The British Legion, successor to the Great War Veterans' Association, held an annual essay competition in the schools on the subject of war and how to prevent it. When I won one of the prizes it seemed natural to think that Dad, who took such an interest in our doings, would attend the presentation. But he would not come: mother was my companion. We sat, as instructed, on the front row. There was some delay in the proceedings. The platform party finally arrived, with the chairman, a former colonel, unsteadily carrying a pile of books up to his chin. He lurched to the table and tried to release his hands from below the books, causing them to billow outward over the table and off the platform. Only after they had been gathered up from the feet of the prize winners and their parents, and the colonel steered back to the bar and replaced, could the presentation, with its lofty theme, begin. Dad listened to my account in silence, seeing nothing funny in it.

Then there were the girls. They began to impose themselves on consciousness as a general background to school and as an incentive to the machismo life of the boys' basement and making the team. While our teachers were trying to open our minds to the learning of the ages our bodies were assuming a manhood we did not know what to do with. Our days and nights could be tantalised with visions of intimacies that were intense but vague and strictly forbidden. Breasts pushed against blouses; what went on in the hearts behind them was a mystery, for having no sisters there was no way of knowing how girls felt. Responses to these newly burgeoning contours could occur at highly inopportune moments, especially embarrassing when suddenly called upon by the teacher to stand up and answer a question.

There was of course absolutely no suggestion of any kind of sex education. In discussions of sex among our peers the level of discourse was very varied, from that of the pretended sophisticate who set the tone, to the innocent like myself who could only listen and marvel both at the information provided and how it was acquired. There were boys who conjectured to my astonishment about the sex life of our teachers, especially the younger females. Such boys spoke of a mysterious substance, Spanish Fly, which would drive a girl crazy for you, though it was never explained how this marvel would always work to the direct and exclusive benefit of the dispenser. One boy insisted that he could tell if a girl was a virgin by the way she walked: he had also made himself, by close observation, an authority on girls' armpit hairs. Another exhibited a Durex condom in its somewhat dogeared envelope. But these boys were not among the brightest in the class: they were trying to trade their dubious knowledge for esteem. Moreover these self-appointed pundits could not be cross-examined without revealing the depths of one's own ignorance.

How could one really find out about such things? Scouring the dictionary for clues was of little use; its demureness was simply maddening. Encyclopaedias, though fuller, were icily clinical. The bible seemed a legitimate source, especially in the light of the dire warnings it contained. But secret attempts to penetrate the coded language of the Old Testament were no great help, though it was some relief to learn that men in general, even the great King David, so noble in his youth, were driven by the flesh. Passages in the Song of Solomon seemed to express something of what one felt, but the eastern imagery was all wrong for bouncing Canadian girls in fresh calico. Occasionally there were glimpses of *The Calgary Eyeopener* (the nearest thing to soft porn available), but it was not allusiveness that was reqired, but the realities on which such allusiveness was based. The anthropological tack was hardly more rewarding. Rifling through the *National Geo-*

graphical Magazine in the school library produced articles on Africa where were to be found the only available depictions of naked breasts, but the result was disappointment and even revulsion as the female form was shown beyond its prime. The movies, under the strict eye of the Hays Office, stopped far short of what you needed to know. The Minister at First Baptist, no doubt recalling his own confusions and tortures, delivered a sermon on the difference between 'eros' and 'agape', with much emphasis on the innocence of the latter but with a moving cloud of evasion surrounding the former. At no point did our parents enter directly into this area of perplexity, longing and inhibition. We were expected to live lives that were clean in mind and body; sex was unclean except within marriage, and even there dubious. Father once said in an unwontedly cryptic manner, 'When a man marries he will know whether his wife is a virgin'. This remark, so clearly an effort of will on his part, was recognised as such by us. It was so intensely embarrassing to him and to us that, promising though it was in one sense, to pursue it required more courage than we possessed. Meanwhile the girl-centred fantasies of adolescent summers increased in wilfulness, sweeping through one with appalling intensity of feeling.

But there was another side to all this. It centred upon Enid Dunbar. She was something remote, almost sacred, standing high above the physiology of sex and surrounded with a kind of nimbus of innocent warmth. Beneath her golden-red hair was a pair of periwinkle blue eyes, and lower still a ready smile revealing gapped teeth with a tiny V of gum between them. Perhaps she was a little on the heavy side, but in my eyes this did not detract from an almost ethereal quality. But she was unattainable. She was a year older than I, an almost insurmountable barrier in high school terms. She was also of a different social stratum, the daughter of a doctor whose friends were among the professional and business classes, living in a free-standing house, the kind of girl who in due course would be presented to the Governor General as a debutante, with her picture in the paper. The boys in her circle had cars that would take them to Tesky's at Hog's Back and other such places where money could be spent. She was a member of that relatively small group in the school who could confidently expect to go to University at their fathers' expense.

I was torn between worshipping from afar (a pleasant and riskless activity), and the urge to make contact (with no very clear idea of what to do next). We shared the last three blocks on the way to Lisgar. It became an obsessive concern to time a convergence. But she was an erratic performer, making the thing a complete lottery. When her father died suddenly I desperately wanted to say something to her, but courage failed. When the Oxford Group came to Ottawa, holding meetings in the Chateau Laurier, she attended. I took this to be a hopeful sign, for I felt I knew something about religion, and father had interviewed Frank Buckman the founder of the Group and had expounded its beliefs and practices to us, giving me a special expertise. Making my way home from First Baptist one evening in the snow and walking past her door, I was seized by a kind of madness. I resolved on the desperate course of calling on Enid. She was out. But her widowed mother, in the expectation that she would be home soon, invited me in. The baffled lady had never heard of me, but she behaved admirably, seeking for leads. I found myself conducting two conversations, one with Mrs. Dunbar and the other in my head with Enid should she arrive and find me there. The Dunbars were of Scottish descent and had visited Edinburgh: we discoursed about Princes Street, the Castle and the Forth Bridge. Somehow we passed on to sermons. I had recently heard Dr. Woodside, the minister of Chalmers United Church where the Dunbar's attended, preach on the text 'And the Tekoite nobles put not their necks into the building of the wall', and introduced this as a topic. We agreed on the Reverend Doctor's erudition and powers of discourse. By this time a kind of desperation was enveloping me. I excused myself, struggled into my galoshes and overcoat and left. For weeks afterwards my efforts were directed towards avoiding Enid, so deep was my embarrassment. I resolved that distance was safer. Enid for her part took no action.

Hitler came to power in January 1933. Shortly afterward at school, as the hubbub was subsiding to let morning assembly begin, the Principal made his way down the aisle with a strange man in tow. We had a visiting speaker! Then came a *frisson*. It was our Dad. He had carefully given no hint. When he was seated in triumph on the school stage we could see him looking about trying to locate us. What on earth was he going to talk about? We were paralysed with a fear of catastrophe. The Principal announced the speaker's name and identity, attracting to us elbows and glances from classmates, and then said that he would tell us what Hitler's victory at the polls would mean to Germany and the world. With growing relief we listened as Dad pondered what the new Chancellor stood for. There was none of the table-banging dogma we knew so well at home. Dad was, of course, a radical liberal, hostile to charismatic leadership except in a liberal form, and deeply distrustful of Germany with its militaristic past. He also fervently believed that a nation, like an individual, had to stand up for the right: the resolution passed in the Oxford Union that its members would not fight for King and Country had aroused his deep indignation. But he gave a carefully balanced account. There was generous applause from the school, not altogether due to being rescued from the first class of the day and its attendant homework.

Afterwards as I entered Miss Murray's classroom she said in her authoritative and highly audible way: 'You have reason to be proud of such a father'. Later, in order not to reveal that we were indeed proud, we taxed him, while speaking, with holding his hands together across his now expanding stomach. He took this seriously: 'How should I stand?' he asked, 'Like this, or this?' trying various dispositions of hands and arms. We reported to mother Miss Murray's remark: it was the best way of conveying our pride, free of embarrassment, to father.

CHAPTER 10

Our Immortal Souls

Whereas our parents had no part in High School, in religion it was otherwise. It was father who set our spiritual ambience, with our mother's concurrence. He committed us to an entire tradition of belief, as well as to a particular setting for it, namely First Baptist Church. The faith of John Bunyan as father held it, demanded a strenuous but not a blind dedication of mind and soul. It rejected the easy acquiescence that forebore to test the faith by questioning and which felt no compulsion to convert others. How was a young mind, cast in such a setting, to find itself? How was one to come to terms with the twin demands for faith combined with rational conviction, together with a public display of these, 'bearing witness' in an Anglo-Scots society in which overt demonstrations of such a kind were not welcome, and were, indeed, likely to be deeply embarrassing?

All this was compounded by the dawning in early teenage of the realisation that the 'firm foundations' of our faith, celebrated in the hymnal, had been called in question since Victorian times. They were, we gradually realised, threatened by the German higher criticism concerning the provenance of the Bible and the claims for it as the literal word of God, and by Darwinian notions of the creation and the evolution of man. Occasionally one of the more liberal professors of theology from McMaster University, founded by a fundamentalist Baptist Senator, would appear in our pulpit. The questioning young mind could quickly perceive in such men a guardedness about such matters, together with a good deal of muting of many passages of Scripture. Dad, of course, had known since his young manhood of these debates, and had been deeply troubled by them. He was one of the many victims of the split in the mind of the evangelical nonconformist. He had embraced the stripping away of ritual and imagery in the belief that his Christianity would stand up to any amount of rational scrutiny. This belief rested on his confidence that when the argument reached to ultimates, including the soul and God, science would be exhausted, admit its limitations, and leave the field to faith. Rationalism was thus no threat to belief, but was its handmaiden, and a humble one at that. And yet, if the Bible was indeed a human collage, containing what seemed to be inconsistencies, together with dreadful Old Testament brutalities not only condoned but set in motion by a God who could appear as capricious as any in the Greek or Teutonic pantheons, and if the Genesis story of creation had to yield place to an evolutionary man acquiring a soul somewhere along the way, how much damage did this inflict upon the old faith? How far could tentativeness and eclecticism be reconciled in minds framed in a tradition of assertive certainty beginning with the protestant reformation and sealed with the blood of its martyrs?

Lisgar Collegiate and First Baptist Church were separated only by Cartier Square, a large empty open space where games were played. But high school and church were kept sharply apart in our lives. School was one thing: church was another. For though our preachers were never tired of saying that religion and life were one, this was most definitely not so. One high school kid hardly knew the religion of another, except for the Jews who had their special holidays. Moreover the principles of selection for school and church were different. The church, in spite of regularity of attendance, produced no intimate friends either for me or my parents.

High School drew upon a representative sample of the population of all of the children of our part of the city: in it they were all subjected to the concept held of education by the Province of Ontario. Each denomination of church, on the other hand, contained its own distinct group of people, each believing to greater or lesser degree that it possessed a unique level of religious (and therefore universal) truth. The personal composition of each was determined to a high degree by the hereditary succession of family tradition, much of it, as in our own case, derived from the Old Country and its complex religious history. A selective process had operated, the origins of which were largely forgotten by those whose religious lives were regulated by it, a process that had played a compelling role in the lives of England, Wales, Scotland and Ireland since at least the seventeenth century. It is true that a group of Canadian protestant denominations (the Presbyterians, Methodists and Congregationalists) had discovered in 1925, after much debate, that their agreements were greater than their differences and had come together in the United Church of Canada. But such unions always leave behind fragments of the original churches who cling compulsively to their differences for fear of betraying the beliefs of their forebears and imperilling their souls. Moreover there were those who could not assimilate, including the Baptists and the Unitarians. In addition new, especially evangelical, sects appeared from time to time, trying to reach back to what they conceived to be the primitive simplicity of the Apostles, and challenging all other churches to join them in this renewal. Meanwhile the Anglican Church proceeded placidly on its way with much establishment support, and the Roman Catholic Church rested on the dual but conflicting loyalties of the French and the Irish with their distinct traditions.

Father had wholeheartedly agreed when the Baptists had held out stubbornly in 1925 for their own identity, declining to join the new United Church of Canada. Adult baptism by total immersion was, he believed, what the Scriptures and Christ demanded of anyone seeking to join the Christian church. Of infant baptism he was scathing, demanding to know what it could possibly mean to sprinkle a child. He would make fun of the mechanics of so doing, ignoring the fact that adult total immersion could be even more open to jokes and parody.

Our baptistry was a little like a Punch and Judy show. It was high up on the right-hand side of the church, a hole in the panelling shaped like a procenium arch, with green baize curtains that drew aside to reveal the actors within, visible from the waist upward, clothed in robes of white. At the age of twelve I appeared on this elevated, water-based stage for the few seconds required for total immersion. There were two perspectives on the scene. That enjoyed by the congregation was solemn and reverential with an uplifting sense of sin washed away. As each candidate was laid backward under the water the choir and congregation chanted

> At the Cross, at the Cross,
> Where I first saw the light
> And the burden of my sin rolled away

But behind the pannelling the atmosphere was quite different, being one of nervous tension and high emotion battling with a physical reality in which so much could go wrong. Total immersion, for all its high symbolism, is difficult to carry out, being haunted by the dangers of bathos. I am not quite sure why Eddie and I were there that Sunday evening in this mixed company of men and women awaiting a renewal of life when life for us was still so new. We had been 'prepared' by sessions in the vestry with one of the senior deacons, whose grasp of the arguments for baptism had not impressed us. It was his job to instruct us as initiates in the secrets of the faith, the catechism, and to discover if we were 'ready'. We were not told that baptism was the initial rite or sacrament of Christianity, taking the place of circumcision among the Jews. Somewhat vaguely we were offered the prospect of a numinous, transcendent experience of being born again. In a way his affirmative verdict on our preparedness was the right one. We had indeed been imbued by sermons and Sunday School with the appropriate sense of sin (perhaps exaggerated by the confusions of puberty), together with the corresponding urge to minimise the punishment therefore. But a kind of light-heartedness and perhaps light-headedness kept breaking through, making me aware of a conflict between a feeling of pending redemption and a sense of the ridiculous.

By the time we were assembled to don our shining robes I was in a state of mild hysteria, with a much heightened sense of what was going on around me. The Reverend Albert came pounding up the stairs to climb into a vast black rubber outfit like that of a diver, reaching up to his chest, slipped its straps over his shoulders and struggled into his robe. He splashed down the marble steps of the baptistry and composed himself behind the green curtains. A nod to the attendant deacon caused the curtains to be pulled gently aside so that our latter-day John the Baptist was revealed to the congregation. 'At the Cross' floated up to us from below; we were lined up in order of appearance. When your turn came you made your way carefully down the steps, counting as you had been told. The water became much cooler as you descended into the marble-lined tomb, a striking lesson in physics. You used one hand to stop your robe from billowing out on the water like a crinoline. The minister, who seemed so composed from afar, was visibly nervous at the complicated manoeuvres required of him. As my head went under and I entered into the new life there was a momentary consciousness of the minister's impure breath.

But though there was a stubborn belief among Baptists of the rightness of their central tradition, the world moved relentlessly on, confronting even them with new challenges. Dr. Maplin the minister of our childhood had been much in the nineteenth century tradition that did not stray far from the divine inspiration of the Bible and a more or less literal interpretation of what it said. If he knew of the implications of Germanic higher criticism, treating the Scriptures as subject to scientific textual scrutiny, he gave no sign. The adolescent mind found the old literalism hard to take and indeed sometimes comical. How could the hairs of your head possibly be numbered: what would the use of such data be except perhaps to the manufacturers of hair tonic? The mechanics of Noah and his hopelessly congested ark were wildly improbable, a rich field for jokes: how did Noah stop the animals at the top of the food chain from munching their way down it, and if he did, how did he save them from starvation? What was all this sentimentality about sheep, such stupid animals? Especially the one who showed the supreme idiocy of wandering away from the ninety and nine: there could be no Darwinian principle of increasing intelligence if such strays were not allowed to breed out.

Dr. Maplin's approach reappeared in our pulpit from time to time when visiting or relief preachers occupied it, often ageing men. To a teenager there was a curious mixture of impatience and sympathy listening to such a patriarch, his faith no longer so urgent as when he first heard the call when it could be infused with the passion of youth. He would labour through the points of his sermon, falling back on slack clichés, but feeling the need to end on a rising note of exhortation. He would throw the burden from the brain to the lungs and heart, a strain made manifest in a purple and perspiring face. As the adrenalin thus summoned worked its effect a little of the fading vision would be briefly restored by auto-intoxication, the pounding of the pulpit would establish a rhythm so that at the climax self-doubt would be drowned in the torrent of words and justification would be temporarily complete. But as he stood at the church door to shake hands with the congregation he would seem curiously shrunken, pale with the expanded effort.

There was a deep sense of embarrassment as it began to dawn on me that such sermons and prayers, for all their surface positiveness, were the pleading by adult men with a yearning for security, for identity and for escape from the fear of oblivion. There seemed to be an inverse relationship between the intensity and insistence of such utterances and the belief really reposed in them. There was, too, the terrible intellectual paucity of so many sermons as they struck the adolescent mind being opened up in high school to the nature of rational thought and the tenable forms of proof.

Dr. Maplin was succeeded by the Reverend Sayles. His tenure was brief and lacked definition, though he did seize upon the Ottawa earthquake of 1925 as the basis of a sermon on the need for mankind to be aware of the precariousness of its existence. There followed a lengthy search for a successor. The choice of the deacons fell upon the Reverend Robert Albert.

He was tall and slim, with silver-grey hair sleekly brushed straight back from a face handsome in the intellectual manner. Beautifully dressed, usually in grey, he had an attractive voice modulated in the cultured English fashion. His sermons were very different from those of Dr. Maplin, resting on a wide grasp of literature and enlivened with a deft wit. There was a controlled sense of drama that brought especially the Old Testament stories to life: when he spoke of Agag 'walking delicately' almost imperceptible mimetic movements of his body brought Agag before us. He was splendid on occasions of high emotion, as on Armistice Sunday. He knew how to keep the pulpit at a distance from the congregation by assuming the full dignity and remoteness of the preachers role; he also knew when and how to induce a sense of intimacy, as for example soon after arrival he told the congregation that the colours of his English academic hood were the same as those of the Ottawa Senators hockey team.

But there was a kind of blandness that troubled some of the older members of the church. He did not enter, in his sermons, into theological travails, nor did he invite contemplation of the dark night of the soul. He did not gratuitously offend the wealthier members of the church by labouring the difficulties confronting the rich man who sought to enter the Kingdom of Heaven. The status of the Bible as the word of God was not brought under scrutiny: its marvellous stories were taken at face value.

On the other hand he had an urge for colour and ritual. He desired, in contrast to the older Baptist manner of service, so devoid of ceremonial, that there should be a processional entry and exit by the choir supported by the organ, that there should be anthems and a set of responses between minister and congregation of an almost liturgical kind, and that the entire service should be a smooth and unified flow. This, combined with the drawing power of his sermons, would make it possible to raise the status of First Baptist from its relative obscurity to a fashionable down-town church. Indeed he had already had some success, with one of his services being paid the compliment of a broadcast when that facility was still new.

But the interior layout of the church was unsuitable for this change in worship, and so would have to be redesigned and restructured. Indeed it would need to be reoriented from an east-west axis to a north-south one. The Reverend Albert seeing himself in the role of the great bishops who had raised the finance for the splendid cathedrals of Europe, set about remaking his church and its services. This, however, required a good deal of money. The deacons, of whom father was one, were thus confronted with two challenges, did they want such revolutionary changes, and how were they to be paid for? The Reverend Albert carried the day, in spite of deep misgivings on the part of some.

The money question he solved partly by appeal to the congregation and partly by seeking a patron. He found it in the Lindsay Thomas family, lumber and sawmill barons. They had been Baptists for generations, ardent founders of Baptist churches, setting up at least six in the Ottawa Valley. The minister proposed a stained-glass window to commemorate John Cameron Thomas and John A. Lindsay, two deceased uncles of Lindsay Thomas, himself a deacon. At this point father rebelled and ceased to be a deacon. 'If the Lindsay Thomas family wants a memorial to itself', he declared, 'let them pay for it themselves!'

The highlight of the celebrations of the remaking of the interior of the church was the unveiling of the window over the gallery at the north end. The Reverend Albert had persuaded John Buchan, Lord Tweedsmuir, to unveil it. When we took our seats in our pew there in front of the pulpit stood an enormous brass eagle lectern, borrowed from Christ Church Cathedral, from which the Governor-General was to read the lesson. A rustle and murmuring at the back of the church announced the vice-regal party and His Excellency made his way down the centre aisle. The creator of Richard Hannay and Sandy Arbuthnot and the student of Augustus Caesar and Oliver Cromwell was a surprisingly small man whose springy gait suggested he was walking on sponges. When the time came he stepped forward and pretty well disappeared behind the eagle, his thin tenor voice, cleared of most of its Scottish origins, an almost disembodied sound.

The window when unveiled consisted of three lancets, with Christ in the middle one, flanked by two lumberjacks, one with an axe and the other with a peavy. Underneath these clearers of the forest cover of the Ottawa Valley was the text, 'The Trees of the Wood sing out in the Presence of the Lord' (Chronicles I). The Reverend Albert must have been fairly desperate in his search of the Biblical lexicon to produce so inept a text. But he had achieved his aim, a remodelled church, more fitting for his idea of worship.

The Reverend Albert's faculty for drama was not yet exhausted. At a morning service not long after the unveiling he produced the mortgage deeds of the church and announced that the debt had been paid off. He then placed the document in a salver on the communion table and set it alight. This was the only time that fire rather than water was the centre of attraction in First Baptist.

In a sense the congregation was not so grateful as it might have been. One old lady, perhaps soured by the effect of the Reverend Albert on a high proportion of the female part of the congregation, left in dudgeon, exclaiming 'They are trotting Church of England as fast as they can go.' At a less outspoken level a certain sense that the minister's sermons were lacking in 'power' gained ground. By this was meant, I suppose, that he did not agonise over the nature of the soul, punishment, redemption and death, the strong meat of the Baptist tradition, refusing to dwell among the *tenebrae*, but provided instead a blue-sky ministry presented in an urbane and reassuring manner. The old Baptist spirit that had animated Prime Minister John A. Macdonald, the dour Scottish stonemason who had laid the cornerstone of the church, lived on among an element of the congregation. Perhaps fate had misplaced the Reverend Albert: the latitudinarianism of the Church of England, with its prospects of a bishopric, would have suited him better.

His successor was the Reverend Scott Evening. He represented the rising young generation, only two years out of McMaster with his B.A., B.D., tall, earnest with flashing rimless glasses and a perhaps too ready smile, happily married, with a reliable helpmate and young children. He was serious in a way that some suspected the Reverend Albert was not, seeing Christianity as a universal cure for the ills of the world, but steady and reasonable. He was able to find his way through the new liberal theology that was the product of the new Biblical scholarship and the rising tide of evolutionary biology and geology and anthropology that threatened the older fundamentalism. He was able to introduce into his sermons the idea that the Bible was to a degree a historically and culturally determined set of documents, but could insist that in some overall sense the hand of God was behind it. He was free both of the ponderousness of Dr. Maplin and of the dangerous charisma of the Reverend Albert, providing, respectively, a concession to youth and a reassurance to the deaconate who judged that he could be kept from extravagance of utterance or action. In a sense these three men reflected the challenges confronting a congregation whose beliefs concerning church government made each congregation autonomous and independent, requiring it, before God, without the aid of bishops or presbytery, to find its own way.

It was the deacons who were, in the first instance, charged with this responsibility. They served as sidesmen welcoming the congregation, guiding strangers to their seats, taking up the offertory and conferring in regular deacon's meetings with the minister. They were largely of the middle bourgeoisie, consistent with the history of their dissenting sect. Karl Marx would have hated them. Somehow each of them had made a favourable impression on the congregation such as to cause their selection to office. There were those among them who were drab and uninteresting whom even Dickens would have found difficult to infuse with colour. But there were also those whose performance we watched with interest. There was the Admiral, a tiny man with a fiery countenance whom we saw in imagination on the quarter-deck flying his flag. On one splendid occasion after the church had been remade and the pew-ends raised, the Admiral, in taking up the collection, having reached the front of the church in full view, struck one of the projections with his collection plate, scattering the contents far and wide, but retaining the plate. Discipline told: the Admiral did not grovel, but with his countenance at the apoplectic level, continued with his task, tendering his almost empty plate to the minister to be blessed among the others. Mr. Bamforth was a thin and withdrawn man with an artificial leg, who carried great weight with his fellow deacons, being one of those men who in a discussion could make his silences heard until the rest solicited his opinion. At the other physical extreme was Mel Mayer, wholesale butcher, a man of great girth, good hearted but without intellectual pretensions. Father repeatedly asked him why it was impossible to buy English pork pies in Canada, but received no satisfactory answer. Mr. Cedar ran a florist business, his gardens being adjacent to the principal cemetery. Mr. Whitehouse was known to be the shadow of his wife: through him her voice was vicariously heard in the deacon's meetings. Our rich man, Mr. Lindsay Thomas, we knew from Christ himself would, with his faultless tailoring and immaculate spats, and in spite of the memorial window, have as much chance of getting into heaven as a camel through the eye of a needle. With much better prospects was Mr. Pearman, by far the most senior of the deacons and probably the poorest, a tiny wizened man who sat alone at the far end of our pew. Like Christ he had been a carpenter, with the second finger of his left hand missing to prove it. He dated from long ago, born when Ottawa had been Bytown.

A perennial worry for the deacons was the Sunday School, held in the basement of the church. Church basements and school basements had a good deal in common. Both were places where important but secondary functions were performed. Both contained the lavatories, the boiler room and the janitor. The basic function of the church basement was the Sunday School. In our case there was a largish open space, with rooms that could be closed off by movable partitions of frosted glass along one side and the back. There was also a room containing the remains of a children's library, a remote relic of an attempt to guide children's reading. The school began and ended with general hymn singing and prayer in the open space, with the middle portion of the service occupied with Bible study classes behind the glass partitions. The teacher would use a lesson aid provided by an American Baptist organisation, treating Biblical interpretation at a pretty simple level.

We discovered as we got older that the teacher could easily be thrown by the implications of some of the stories, especially from those of the Old Testament. It was hard to comprehend the Lord's dealings with the Israelites; why should an omnipotent and omniscient God involve himself with so wilful a people? If with all that divine concern and all those prophets to point the way they so often went wrong and required chastisement, why did God persist, knowing, as He was presumed to do, the outcome? When the Ark of the Covenant was tottering on its ox-cart and a man stretched out his hand to steady it he was struck dead—what kind of a God was that?

Because the growth of the city meant a loss of downtown population there was the general worry that the congregation would shrink. This made recruitment through the Sunday School important. Moreover, there would be concern from time to time whether the church was reaching the working classes and their young. First Baptist thus shared the dilemma of all evangelical churches, namely that, being so completely middle class, how was it to discharge the function assigned to it by Jesus of taking the Gospel to all men and women, especially the less economically and socially fortunate? Such people could never really enter into the life of the church, contributing without embarrassment to its social life, its choir, its men's Bible class and its finances.

At about the same time as the new minister, Mr. Baker, a rising civil servant of youngish middle age, arrived. He quickly became a deacon. Knowing something of the settlement movement in London and Chicago, he argued that what was needed was a boys' club meeting on Wednesday evenings. 'If you have a good programme', he insisted, 'the boys will come'. The thing got off to a quite promising start, Ed and I attending. But then something seemed to go wrong with the supervisory arrangements. One Wednesday night no adult at all turned up. There was a period of hanging about, developing into mild horseplay. Then someone produced a rugby ball. It was thrown from one to another for a time, the chairs in the hall being pushed and piled back. Then came drop kicking, careful at first, then gaining in abandon until a misdirected shot hit the Sunday school clock. It was an ornate affair high on the wall, surrounded by complex carvings. The face by some miracle was not damaged, but the carvings dropped away onto the floor. This should have sobered us, but instead induced a kind of hysteria of merriment. Someone suggested that we should all go and explore the church above. God's house, as it was often referred to in sermons, was dark and cavernous, very quiet and still, full of brooding shadows. It created a new mood. Instead of the boisterousness of the basement there came over us a sense of mystery, almost of fear. But the two leading spirits of this escapade, not of the church membership, were not to be easily suppressed. They began climbing about the pews, entering the choir stalls and posturing in the pulpit. To see them cavorting where the minister had invoked the Almighty, where the choir had sung its anthems and where the communion had been dispensed, was too much. We suddenly felt ashamed and frightened, remembering the terrible Old Testament punishments for sacrilege. There was a concerted movement to go home, leaving our alien leaders with no followers.

For the most part there was little zealotry at First Baptist. A burning urge to convert at all costs was hardly consistent with the bourgeois spirit of the place. We had no Savonarola calling with the zeal of obsession for the purging of society of its sins and sinners. The European wars of religion were seen as misguided struggles conducted in a remote and barbarous age, now long passed, superceded by a genial climate of religious toleration.

For these reasons the arrival of Neil McDougall came as a profound shock. He was new from Scotland, a rabid fundamentalist evangelical, consumed with the fires of conversion and a hatred of the Roman Catholic Church. Strong though father's anti-Catholicism was, that of this man trembled on the edge of madness. In spite of this Neil was welcomed as a Sunday School teacher, of which there was never an excess supply. He was one of those men who, though ultimately at the mercy of his obsessions, could keep these under control when dealing with deacons or Sunday School superintendents. He was the more disturbing because there was a curious perverse rationality about him: he stood for our basic evangelical beliefs carried to the ultimate insensitivity that had caused Savonarola and the wars of religion: he was a living *reductio ad absurdam*. He dilated at length on the sins of the Popes, having made a special study of their carnal delinquency. He would walk us along the wall of the Gloucester Street Convent telling us of the perversions that he imagined went on inside. 'What kind of man is it', he would ask of the Catholic priesthood, 'who could hold in his own hands what he believed to be the literal body and blood of Christ?' He revelled in condemnation of the dark world of priests and nuns (giving them a strange hieratic power over my mind). The Catholic world was for him a kind of Gothic horror, with its high convent and monastery walls, its guttering candles, its incantations, its agonised figures of Christ expiring on His Cross, together with the secret intimacies of the confessional. Poor Neil was, indeed, only a step removed from those men who encased themselves in sandwich boards and walked the streets warning of impending doom, except that he had the guile to know when and in what quarters not to make his obsessions apparent, giving it full rein among the boys. None of this, of course, did we convey to our parents.

Neil, in order to correct abuses and to spread the true religion, expected us to urge salvation on perfect strangers, pressing upon them the religious tracts with which he supplied us in great quantities. Each tract bore a coloured picture of Christ (looking not all that different from Catholic pictures, except that the Sacred Heart was not exposed), together with the story of a dramatic and lasting conversion that had raised the person recounting it from the depths of despair and often degradation to become, almost instantaneously, a useful member of society and the centre of a happy family.

Instinctively we had our reservations about the efficacy of the tracts. Even more plainly we were aware of the dangers of confronting strangers in this way. Perhaps Neil thought our youthful innocence would protect us. But it was not physical fear that beset us, but that of rebuff and ridicule. Worst of all was the dread that news of our activities as tract distributors might reach our school-fellows. So we did the best we could—leaving tracts behind in the street car or in the movies and in desperation stuffing quantities of them into public mail boxes. Each Sunday Neil asked us how many we had disposed of and eagerly replenished our stocks. He announced that there would be a prize for the champion distributor. My older brother to his intense embarrassment and stricken conscience, was the winner, having a eulogy pronounced over him in Sunday School class. The prize was a bound volume of tracts.

This zealous man did not confirm our belief, but rather added to our doubts. So reservations began to accumulate. We were taught that all men and women were basically the same as they came from the hand of God and depended upon Him. It followed that cultural differences, however seemingly deep, were superficial and that the Christian Gospel provided the right set of beliefs for all men. This was the philosophy that lay behind Christianising missions, ignoring the fact that Christianity itself, with its many sects, was highly conditioned by history and culture. The earnest missionaries on furlough or in retirement who addressed us in Sunday School seemed to emanate a blind optimism that bordered on simple-mindedness. The hymns we stood and sang gained in incongruity as we got older: a feeling of inanity came over you as you solemnly joined others in wishing to be washed in the blood of the lamb. We did not know any exotic peoples in the flesh, but we did encounter them in our reading: there was for example Sir Walter Scott's Saladin, the noble foe of the Crusaders, whom it would have been a fearful presumption to try to convert from the faith he defended against the Christian adventurers.

And yet, in spite of so much questioning, though the anchor dragged, the chain did not break. It was urged upon us as a central tenet that religion was the prime source of one's identity, the true basis of self. From this there appeared to be no escape. Secular, humanist man, it seemed, was bound to lose his way; morality could not stand for long without a basis in belief that went beyond man. For all the *ennui* of Sunday when secular entertainment was all but shut down, even the young could be brought to see the case for a time of contemplation, for pondering one's stewardship and for the restoration of a true perspective on life. The trouble with this, however, was that it could lead to morbidity, for before very long you arrived at man's mortality and the fear of death: these were the real sources of Sunday gloom.

In one sense we were embarrassed by our Baptist peculiarities. But in another we were proud of them. We rejected the idea that our beliefs were derivative in the sense of arising merely as a reaction to the distortions, abuses and accretions of Roman Catholicism, but claimed it to be the pristine faith and practice of the disciples. We liked to think we were the heirs of the early church, whose progenitors had somehow preserved the faith in obscure places in Asia Minor, in direct lineal descent from St. Paul and innocent of the terrible things that had been done by organised religion in the long intervening years, especially under the Papacy. We applauded people like H.G. Wells who wondered what Christ would think if he returned and saw gaudy interiors, heavily bedecked priests and painted images, all illumined by candles and infused with incense, forgetting that Wells was an enemy of all religions including our own.

But though the anchor held through the teenage years, there was also a sense of guilt, sometimes agonising, of not being able to believe without reservation, of not being able to control a certain cynicism, and of being desperately unwilling by impertinent advocacy to tamper with the belief systems of others that we were told were mistaken. In any case the worst of aberrations, that of Roman Catholicism, could be held by such excellent people, including my closest friend Jon Flynn, and all his family. Jon was an altar boy, assisting in the Mass, perpetuating ritualist superstition, and yet he was the most down-to-earth among us. We were taught to abhor the zealotry that had brought the carnage of the wars of religion, and yet to admire the steadfastness of the Cromwellians and the Covenanters and not to regret the splitting of Christendom into factions. A liberal belief in broadmindedness and tolerance hardly fitted with a feeling of admiration, and indeed envy, for the Old Testament prophet-zealots who could denounce and call down the wrath of God like an artillery barrage.

It was mostly on Sundays, with their two services together with Sunday School, that these tortured thoughts moved to the forefront of the mind. On weekdays they receded into the unconscious while what preachers called mundane affairs asserted their supremacy. Only when you put your hand in your pocket and found some of Neil's tracts did the condition of your soul and its prospects for a felicitous immortality suddenly intrude.

CHAPTER 11

England Again, the Wheel has come Full Circle

I left Canada, in September 1938, to attend University in England. In the event I was to make my home in the Old Country, although the voices across the water never failed to call me back to Canada, especially in spring when the ice was breaking on the river and the air was filled with the promise of summer.

Although I was immediately excited at the prospect of an ocean voyage and of becoming a full-time student it was a sombre leave taking. Father was full of forebodings as Europe again stumbled towards war. At nearly sixty years of age with little prospect of a comfortable retirement, he was seriously depressed, perhaps thinking forward to the prospect of losing a son to another war. But mother, although herself still battling with illness, said, 'Go, the future lies before you'. She died in 1941. I never saw her again.

As the ship ploughed its way across the Atlantic and I tried to learn to knit, taught by a charming fellow passenger, less optimistic spirits might have wondered what the future held. It was the week of Munich when Neville Chamberlain brought back his 'Peace with Honour' Agreement with Adolf Hitler. Although none were to recognise it at the time Chamberlain by gaining a year's respite may have cost Hitler the war by giving the British a twelve month in which to begin the process of serious re-armament. But any such considerations were to fade into insignificance at the excitement of attending the University of Birmingham, enrolled, at the age of 22, as a first year undergraduate in the Faculty of Commerce.

It did seem amazing that this transformation should have been possible in view of the prospects facing me in the autumn of 1934, with the Great Depression at its depth, when, at almost 18 years of age I had left school. Getting a job, any job, was the great thing. Parents fretted, perhaps more than their children, as the level of unemployment crept upward. As for opportunity, the class of '34 divided into three groups. A few had the choice of university education and thence of entrée to the professional class from which most of their fathers had

131

23   Ice breaking on the Ottawa River, Spring 1938.

24   On board *The Duchess of Atholl*, learning to knit, September 1938.

25   Sydney George Checkland at home in Ottawa, *c.*1937.

sprung. Those whose parents had sufficient standing and respectability found their children jobs, often as clerks in some office or other. Finally, there were those whose parents could give no help and who might well be still seeking a proper job when the Second World War broke out five years later.

My brother and I did obtain clerkships. He entered a commercial enterprise, I joined the Bank of Nova Scotia in the humblest capacity. Our parents were jubilant. Although we both earned very little, we were poised on the bottom rung of a long, long ladder—stretching it seemed to infinity and indeed retiral. At first this bleak prospect did not alarm me. I entered briskly into the routine of studying for the Associateship of the Canadian Bankers Association. Having attained this objective, there being no promotion in sight, I began to get restless. The years seemed to lie ahead endlessly in a threatening manner. I began to calculate how much would be needed before I could quit and aim for university. It became clear that there could be no adequate savings out of the miserly pay given by the Bank. While my parents agonised about my foolhardiness in giving up a secure job, I resolved to find something to do which would pay more and enable me to save.

I joined a manufacturing concern as accountant and manager in 1936. The pay was good but the risks were high. The business although old established had been in difficulties and had been bought by the new owners who suffered from chronic liquidity problems. As their acountant I found myself using all sorts of devices to delay payment. We regularly slipped the cheques with which we were paying our bills into wrong envelopes and cheerfully posted them, knowing this device would give us several days grace. One might have thought we had no calendar in the office so numerous were the post-dated cheques we sent out. Woe betide any van-man who allowed credit to a customer and came back to the office without every cent of the money due.

Although all this shady business was unwelcome it did allow me to save sums which seemed considerable to me. Being careful not to discuss the matter of business ethics, with Dad, I watched my savings grow. By early 1938 it seemed sensible to enquire at the University of Birmingham as to whether my qualifications from the Ontario Education Board would be acceptable as entrance qualifications. They replied promptly and encouragingly: there would be no difficulty there. I handed in my resignation and prepared to leave my homeland. I had £450.

I returned to Birmingham almost exactly twenty-five years after my father had left. Not only did I have friends (who had failed to make a living in Canada in the Depression) with whom to stay but there was a ready made family awaiting me. Although my father's closest brother James had died, his widow and my cousins were there as they always had been. My father's favourite sister was also still alive although what this elderly spinster thought of this large young Canadian moving carefully through her cluttered home is not known.

Lectures proved stimulating and enjoyable. Three personalities stand out. Professor John George Smith lectured on Economics. He was good and clear but dealt with the 's' sound in a particularly satisfying, sibilant manner. We waited expectantly for a succession of such sounds; 'successive sterling crises' was the sort of phrase we were eager to hear. Sargent Florence was quite different. An urbane man, he lectured on Labour Economics and such like, giving us the benefit of his American experience. He had an American wife who was active in aspects of social work in the city. The other memory is of Gilbert Walker who lectured to us on Transport Economics. Then young and flamboyant he graced our summer 'flannel dances' exotic in a light-weight cream suit. He gyrated with enthusiasm around the dance floor his raft of red hair making him instantly visible.

And there was a girl. In accordance with my usual prudence I took up a place at the back of the raked lecture theatre. She sat at the front. She had honey coloured hair held at the nape of her neck by a shoe lace. When I worked my way around to view her more closely I could not but notice that the right lens of her glasses was cracked, but had somehow revolved in its frame, producing an intriguing oblique effect. I remained an observer for several months being anxious not to put my slender funds in jeopardy. When this became too tantalising I made an approach. As it turned out I could teach her nothing about economy. Like me she brought packed lunches and she rode a bicycle. As a Geography student she produced the most marvellous multi-coloured ink maps and diagrams which made my impatient efforts look terrible. She was in the same non-conformist tradition as that in which I had been raised.

During my first long vacation, that is in the summer of 1939, immediately before the war broke out I determined to see something

26   Sydney Checkland, setting off on a Continental Tour, Summer 1939.

of Europe. Clearly the bicycle was the thing: but I could not ride one. There were some hilarious moments for my fellow students as I grappled with the simple balancing act necessary to master the machine. The bicycle and the youth hostel was the only way on so slender a budget as mine. An Exhibition (prize) of £30 from the University was a wonderful boost to my precarious finances. From Birmingham I cycled to Southampton to board an ocean liner to cross to Cherbourg.

Altogether I cycled some 3,000 miles until I had to hurry home in the face of general European mobilisation against the Germans. My route took me down the west coast of France to Spain, then along the Pyrenees to Andorra, east up the Rhone Valley and across to Switzerland then into the Black Forest of Germany and westward to Paris and from Paris to Rotterdam and so home. In a small garrison town in the Pyrenees I encountered a young French soldier. To start the conversation I asked the inane question, 'Vous êtes Voluntaire?' To which he replied disspiritedly, 'Ah Oui, Voluntaire obligatoire!' So much for the fighting spirit of the French Army.

About a month later, at Freiburg in the Black Forest I was in a Jugendherberge (German youth hostel). The place was full of young Nazis in full cry, elated by the prospect of war. Whereas a British Boy Scout knife had many blades—though none of them lethal—these lads all had what were in effect daggers, heavily emblazoned with Swastikas and other Nazi symbols. Unlike my lethargic French soldier, they had been conditioned to be ready and eager to kill. They were a terrifying lot for a Canadian to whom the killing passion was so remote. There was much table banging with their daggers as they bawled out one of those marching songs which reflect a military culture of many generations. While in the south of France I had acquired a copy of an obscure provincial newspaper. It contained a highly unflattering caricature of Hitler. On crossing the German frontier I was certain it would be confiscated and myself perhaps debarred. The official looked at it, and having consulted a list of forbidden publications, and because of its obscurity, not finding it listed, carefully folded it and returned it to me. I showed it to my fellow youth hostellers. There were looks of astonishment to see their Fuhrer pilloried. But they made no comment, continuing their roistering in honour of Hitler.

The next day there was a grand parade in the town square. It had a barbaric panache as the banners and brass standards were marched on. When the great shouts of 'Heil Hitler' began I edged toward the back of the crowd, for I could not bear to join in. It was to be a terrible task to stop this mad machine of intoxicated people who had shed their human identity, falling victims to a delirium induced by evil leaders.

27   Auberge de Jeunesse, Boulevard Kellermann, Paris, August 1939. Sydney
with Zvi Rogowsky.

At the beginning of my second year in university the war had
started. Student politics were rapidly complicated by the arrival in
Britain of many exiled student groups. As a student politician of sorts,
being elected President of the Guild of Undergraduates (the Students
Union) and eventually of the National Union of Students, I knew
nothing of Marxism and its tactics of penetration and so was not aware
that the Party had its place in student politics. If I had spent less time
in Canada on the arguments surrounding Christianity and more of it
on Marx, I might have been in a better position to know what was
going on. But living in Ottawa had not encouraged enquiry into the
matter of a revolutionary philosophy.

To complicate matters further many of the occupied countries had produced their own National Union of Students within which Marxism battled with Liberalism. These students had no idea on which side their country would end after the war. The Poles were particularly intense. To celebrate one of their great national days they held a ceremony in London in the old Queen's Hall. They, like everyone else, were desperately short of materials. They had set up a 'perpetual flame' as a symbol of the undying spirit of the Polish people. But bathos overtook them as the flame flickered and nearly died. A hand with a bottle of fuel appeared from behind and revived the flame.

It was a hazardous business to fall among the Poles for an evening. I knew no more of liquor, than of Marxism, and so found it difficult to enter into proceedings which usually ended in deep inebriation. On such occasions cavalry dash became the order of the day, recovering the glories of victory amid defeat and exile. The Poles too astonished by their immense eagerness to begin the job of killing Germans. Such implacable hatred gave new depth to what we had been told in high school about the successive partitions of Poland. We knew Poland as a series of maps. These Poles in Britain during the war, far from being the butt of ignorant fun, as at home in the American movies, became heroic figures.

I graduated in 1941. It pleased me that mother knew of my success before she died in October.

It took me some time to reconcile myself to serving in the war. Partly this was on moral grounds and partly it was frustration with the ineptitude of western politicians. Perhaps it was also a residual from all those anti-war essays I had written at school in Ottawa for the League of Nations Society. Moreover on my 1939 cycling trip, I had seen the acres of graves on the Western front at Verdun and elsewhere. It was the imminent threat to Leningrad and Moscow, together with the treatment of the Jews that changed my mind. I tried to join the Canadian forces and offered myself to the Canadian navy. The Canadian navy doctors turned me down on the ground of eyesight. I decided to improve my physical condition by a course of training, then to volunteer for the British army where standards were a good deal lower. Sure enough, this tactic succeeded. I found myself as trooper No. 7955505, in the Royal Armoured Corps undergoing six weeks basic training. About a dozen of us were then selected for the Pre-Officer Training Course. I did well enough to be sent to Sandhurst. There I felt that I really was joining British history, with echoes of Wellington and most of the great commanders since. In spite of the assault courses it was an enjoyable experience, especially when our troop had learned enough drill to be part of the larger parade. Marching

28   On parade, Royal Military College, Sandhurst. Sydney Checkland is the
marker (front line nearest camera) looking straight ahead, Autumn 1942.

around the great parade ground in front of the Colonnaded Old Building, in clockwork precision under the orders of the senior sergeant
major, from one of the guards regiments, was an exhilerating experience.

As the winner at Sandhurst of the Belt of Honour, as the best cadet
in my troop, I could have chosen any one of the British regiments. But
I was eager to transfer to the Canadian Army. This took time and
proved difficult. In the interval I was sent to the Fifth Battalion of the
Manchester Regiment which is noted for its *fleur-de-lis* cap badge. This
pleased me because it was the regiment in which R.H. Tawney, sage
and guru of the Labour Party, had served during the First World War.
After the retreat at Dunkirk in 1940 the battalion had been retrained
as reconnaissance units and equipped with armoured cars. During my
brief career with them we roamed the Yorkshire/Lancashire moors
enjoying the freedom of movement given by our vehicles.

Eventually I was bidden to the depot of the Governor General's
Footguards in the Canadian Army. The Canadian Brigadier was almost

29   Lieut. S.G. Checkland, Governor General's Foot Guards, Autumn 1943.

hostile to this renegade Canadian who marched in with a Manchester Regiment cap badge and threw an energetic and obviously Sandhurst-inspired salute. It gave me the greatest satisfaction to transfer from the Manchester Regiment of the British Army to the Governor General's Footguards in the Canadian Army. In another sense the transfer was important. The honey haired girl had become my wife. Her pay as a wife or indeed her pension as a widow would be very much better as a Canadian.

Despite the proud name of Governor General's Footguards we were now a tank regiment and as we trained in southern England in the spring of 1944 we knew it was for the invasion of Europe that we were waiting. We all enjoyed the exercises in and around Aldershot. On one occasion, and going against orders, we had plunged into a narrow lane and ended up with our tank ruining the soft driveway to a pleasant house. I went in to apologise. Tea was offered to us all and I found myself chatting to Lettice Fisher, widow of H.A.L. Fisher, the historian whose *History of Europe* I had proudly acquired as a prize at Lisgar Collegiate in Ottawa.

As we waited for D day the air filled with rumours as to when it would come and what part we would play. Our Sherman tanks were fitted with enormous exhaust chutes so as to allow their engines to function even in water at considerable depth. In July 1944 (the initial landing had taken place on 6 June), the regiment received its orders. They were top secret, but there was quite a crowd of women round the gates as our Shermans rumbled through them. We were bound for the East India Docks. It was an extraordinary journey rumbling through familiar London scenes with our armament ready for battle. At the Docks we were to embark on an American merchant ship. Just as we were loading one German buzz-bomb suddenly ceased to buzz, which meant it was about to come to earth and explode. When it did, a large part of the American crews, shouting blasphemous expletives, left their ship and us and rushed to the scene. When they returned we resumed driving our tanks aboard.

The vast hold was fitted with chains and shackles for securing the tanks. The American master, convinced that our passage would be smooth, decided it was not necessary to secure our tanks. As the Colonel had feared, it became quite rough as we passed through the widening of the Channel in approaching Normandy, so that the Shermans shifted, damaging some of the chutes.

But soon we were in sight of Arromanches, the Mulberry harbour where we were to land. Normandy was a place of associations. Miss Murray at Lisgar had laboured to teach us the lovely song, 'Ma Normandie'. This was William the Conqueror's Duchy, containing the Bayeux Tapestry with its marvellous depiction of the struggle between Harold the Saxon and William the Norman. Not far to the east was Brittany, home of Jacques Cartier the sea captain who was the first to penetrate Canada by the St. Lawrence Valley. I wondered how many Lisgarites were aboard who found Miss Murray invoked in their memories.

Driving down the steep ramps was a formidable challenge for the drivers. As we entered the shattered remains of the ancient city of Caen there were German posters of Joan of Arc at the stake with the legend 'The English are back!' Where could the inspiration for such an inept appeal have come from with all the bitterness and humiliation of the occupation only now ending? As for Caen itself, we drove through newly made canyons made by the bulldozers through the rubble of the ancient city. Our job was to take up positions round the perimeter of Caen.

Just after we had taken up our allocated places in the defences a German bombardment began. Tanks are uncomfortable containers to sit in for any length of time. The only real course is to stretch out under the tank. Accordingly I crawled under and there met with a shock. It was in the form of smell, the awful sickly odour of human decay. The track of the tanks had accidentally run over a recent German grave. There was a cigarette tin as the youth's memorial. It contained his letters and a number of snapshots. The letters expressed deep concern for his safety, while the photos were chiefly holiday snaps showing him with his family and his cronies; much as would be the contents of the pockets of my own men. It was with a deep sense of interest that one looked at this material, the reflection of a truncated life. We moved the tank forward and placed the tin box, already beginning to rust where we judged the head to be. We presumed that when opportunity offered others would come and provide a decent and permanent memorial. There must have been hundreds of these hurried, shallow buryings.

One of our early casualties was Willie Rushlaw, one of those boys at school who conveyed to us what street-wise knowledge we had learned. It was he who had embellished a number of posters in the area featuring bulldogs with enormous penises, not to speak of the number of To Let notices that received an i in the middle. He died on his motor bike as a despatch rider. Our second casualty was the technical officer. He was the proud possessor of a splendid pair of leather boots, the best in the Regiment. He had been sitting in his jeep supervising while manoeuvring, crashed into a telegraph pole, felling it. Because of the tangle of overhead wires it took a number of other poles with it, one of which fell across the jeep, killing him. His body was wrapped in a grey blanket and bound with wire. From this mummy protruded the famous boots. Several Panzer divisions came at us, but the perimeter held. Then came the time to move to the Normandy *bocage* on the offensive.

The plan was that we should be the northern *upper* part of a pincer movement, the Americans supplying the southern element, closing on Falaise. There was an all-night bombing barrage by American Flying Fortresses, some of which unfortunately fell on Ouvalliers, and the Polish Armoured Division. The men sat about, discussing the morrow. Were we the descendants of Henry V's men on the eve of Agincourt? These were ordinary lads, most of them born in Ottawa within sight of the Gothic Peace Tower and the sound of its carillon bells, some of whom I had known at school. They had assumed a life-or-death duty for reasons that they could hardly explain. They were, now, like all soldiers, chiefly motivated not by grand ideas of right or wrong, but by loyalty to each other as members of the regiment, reinforced by their Canadian roots. There were the same fears and the same bravado. By this time we had had enough casualties to make us all realise the reality of our situation. Two memories stuck with me of the previous action. One was of an infantry man of the Winnipeg Regiment sitting by the roadside holding his almost severed left arm in his right. The other was of a burning Sherman with comrades trying to haul a half-dead man out of the turret, their grip on the man's wrists and hands coming away with the burned flesh.

One of our difficulties had been that it had never been possible to deploy the full regiment of our tanks in England because there was no room, what with farm buildings, villages and towns. 'Pinnochio', our adjutant, had been wounded so that his role fell to me. The Regimental command tank had been specially adapted. The shield that caught the fired shell-cases had been removed. The turret was full of maps and aerial photos, these latter giving 'information overload'. How could one interpret all this in the midst of action? There was always the urge to use the latest technology even if neither appropriate nor well tried. For example the guns had, shortly before leaving England, been fitted with 'stabilisers', intended to keep them at a constant level over uneven ground, the fruit of the electrical theory of feedback then just beginning to be applied, whereby a change in one direction would provoke a compensatory response. Unfortunately this was unsatisfactory so that the muzzles of the guns would 'hunt', that is be made to vibrate. The men soon disposed of these expensive gadgets, throwing them into the roadside ditches. The men preferred manual control in which they had been trained, but within a decade the new marvel had become a practical proposition.

We proceeded a good distance without engaging the enemy, though we passed large numbers of prisoners, many clearly pleased to be out of the war and into Allied hands at last, some having served on the fearful eastern front where the Russians were much less kind to their prisoners. Soon we were on high ground overlooking the Falaise Gap through which were streaming other Germans, intent on escape back to their comrades. At this point the news came through on the wireless that our Brigadier had been killed. Colonel Scott, our regimental commander, was the senior colonel and was therefore called back to army headquarters to assume the Brigadier's command. This meant that I was left with the regimental command tank for several hours. Our second-in-command, a large and impressive man, took over the Regiment on the second day. The Falaise Gap not having been fully closed it was essential to move quickly. The Major stopped our tank to make inquiries of some infantrymen as to what was on the ground generally.

In order to make up the time thus lost we went bucketing forward. We had overlooked the ingenuity of the Germans even in retreat. A Tiger tank lay in front of us, hull down, and thoroughly camouflaged. It sent a shot into our left side, killing the wireless operator. The tank was on fire almost at once. What with the fuel and ammunition it was necessary to get out as fast as we could. The Major started out of the turret. The Panzer machine-gunned him in the shoulder, causing him to drop back into the turret. This was no good; so I put my shoulders under him and heaved. He passed through the turret hatch, reached the ground, and made a dash for a belt of trees. I followed him out as fast as I could. I found myself running across a field of harvested corn. The Panzer's machine gunner was on the alert. He sent a burst into both of my legs. I was able to crawl to one of the small stacks of the harvest that dotted the field. There, after injecting myself with morphine, I spent the night. At some stage I heard the grinding of the Panzer's tracks as it moved away. I hoped against hope it would not see me in my little castle of the farmer's crops.

Such was my war. It was neither long nor heroic but it had had its moments. In the end I was glad to be invalided out of it although it would have been a joyful experience to have been with the lads of the Ottawa Valley when they rode in triumph liberating the Netherlands. For the peoples of the Low Countries those Canadian soldiers have become heroes and legends.

Afterword

When my husband died in 1986 he left the typescript of *Voices across the Water* in an advanced form. He had intended to develop his notes on his work at the Bank, in business at the University and in Normandy more fully, but this was not to be.

Personal names—apart from those of Sydney Checkland's immediate family—have been changed.

Olive Checkland
Cellardyke
Scotland